OVERHEARD . . .

Peter and Paul Lalonde are leaders in providing fascinating, complete and reliable information on the prophetic fulfillments of this generation.

—Hal Lindsey, author, *Late Great Planet Earth*

Peter and Paul will challenge you to live as if Christ were returning tomorrow.

—Jack Van Impe, Jack Van Impe Ministries

This is the most significant new prophecy book since *Late Great Planet Earth*.

—Arno Froese, Midnight Call Ministries

If you want to know what is happening in the world of Bible prophecy you should be reading Peter and Paul Lalonde.

—David Breese, Christian Destiny Ministries

Peter and Paul are on the cutting edge of Bible prophecy today.

—Paul F. Crouch, President, Trinity Broadcasting Network

I thoroughly enjoy Peter and Paul's writings and find them a constant source of information and inspiration.

—Tim LaHaye, President, Family Life Seminars

Peter and Paul's ministry has a vital role to play in awakening the Church to the rapidly unfolding signs of the soon coming of the Messiah.

—Grant Jeffrey, Frontier Research Publications

Like no one else I've met, Peter and Paul Lalonde have the ability to take the prophecies of the Bible and make them completely understandable to those who hear them.

—Pat Matrisciana, Jeremiah Films

I believe that the insights you will gain from Peter and Paul's writings will thrill and amaze you.

—Ray Brubaker, *God's Behind the News*

2000
A.D.

ARE YOU READY?

How New Technologies and Lightning-Fast
Changes are Opening the Door for Satan and
His Plan for the End of the World

PETER AND PAUL LALONDE

THOMAS NELSON PUBLISHERS
Nashville • Atlanta • London • Vancouver

Published in Nashville, Tennessee, by Thomas Nelson, Inc., and distributed in Canada by Word Communications, Ltd., Richmond, British Columbia, and in the United Kingdom by Word (UK), Ltd., Milton Keynes, England.

Scripture quotations are from The Holy Bible, KING JAMES VERSION.

Library of Congress information

Printed in the United States of America

1 2 3 4 5 6 7 QPK 03 02 01 00 99 98 97

Contents

WE DON'T READ PREFACES EITHER!

(BUT PLEASE READ THIS ONE)

If Bible prophecy really is being fulfilled in this generation and these really are the last days, have you ever wondered why God allowed you to live at this climactic moment in history? After all, God could have ordained that you be born at any time, in any century. But He chose for you to be alive today!

Do you ever think about how the prophets dreamed of living on earth in this day? How they would have yearned to see the things that you see? Yet He specifically chose for you, not them, to have a front row seat to His glorious return. Wow!

We believe that God has a reason for everything. We believe that He has placed you in this pivotal time in history for a reason. It may be to win many or just a tough few to the kingdom in these fleeting moments of time. But one thing is for sure, God wants you to understand the excitement and urgency of the time in which you live.

A WHOLE NEW WAY OF LOOKING AT BIBLE PROPHECY

That is what this book is for. We want to help you understand the day in which you live in a way that you never have before. We want to help you see Bible prophecy through brand-new eyes.

You see, for too long, when people have talked about Bible prophecy, they haven't gone far beyond earthquakes, famines, and wars. Now, to be sure, these are pars of the end-time scenario, but there is so much more to God's plan that has been totally overlooked. In fact, we can guarantee you this. You will hear things in this book that you have never heard before. You will consider possibilities that have never been considered. And by the time you are finished, we'll have given you a whole new way of looking at Bible prophecy.

PROPHECY FOR A NEW GENERATION

Now, it's not because we're so smart or so wise. It's because we can see things in our day that no one could have seen before. Things that the prophets couldn't understand. Being students of Bible prophecy, in our mid-thirties, at this exact moment in history gives us the ability to see this world from a very unique vantage point. It means that we not only understand the Scriptures, but we also understand the emerging worlds of virtual reality, cyberspace, and the Net. It means that we see why members of the younger generation are caught up in *Star Trek* and UFO's—and why they're expecting something big to happen! And it means that we can see how this entire planet is being changed and set up for a deception unlike anything prophecy students have ever imagined.

We believe that we have been called into the kingdom at a specific time and for a specific purpose. And that purpose, we believe, is to be your tour guides to the future. We want to show you what's coming down the pipe and when. We want to help you understand that while this world is changing dramatically, the people in it are changing just as quickly.

YOUR TOUR GUIDES TO THE FUTURE

We want to give you a sense of excitement, expectancy, and an understanding of the times in which we live. We want to bring you right up to date, so that you can see God's plan unfold right before your eyes.

It is our sincerest prayer that as you read this book, you'll get a new vision of God and the accuracy of His Word. And if you do, you'll get a whole new understanding not only of our world, but also of the great hope that lies ahead! As Jesus said, "And when these things begin to come to pass, then look up, and lift up your heads; for your redemption draweth nigh" (Luke 21:28).

ON YOUR MARK

_____

_____

_____

_____

_____

_____

_____

_____

_____

_____

_____

_____

_____

_____

_____

"I do windows" is now the motto of a computer consultant, not a housekeeper.

THE MOMENT YOU'VE BEEN WAITING FOR

It's a devastating frustration most of us have faced. We try to remain calm, but in the face of such adversity it's almost impossible to do. Of course, we're speaking of those occasional weekend mornings when you roll over in bed, reach for the TV clicker, and find that its batteries have died in the night!

If there are no fresh batteries in the nightstand, there are only two choices. Get up for the day, or roll over and go back to sleep. The whole idea of getting up, walking over to the TV, standing there until you find something to watch, and then committing yourself to watching that same channel, through all of the commercials, is out of the question.

Imagine telling someone twenty-five years ago that this day would come. A day when a grown man would rather stare in frustration at the ceiling than be faced with such an untenable circumstance. As you lie there you can almost hear your father giving you his "when I was your age" speech.

Or imagine telling someone a hundred years ago about

this predicament: "Sure, I can get pictures sent right into my bedroom so that I can watch a presidential address, a football game, or a thirty-minute commercial about an exercise machine."

"Wow!" they'd say. "That's amazing."

"Yeah, I guess it is, but if I have to walk across the room to turn it on, it really isn't worth it!"

Ours is a generation that has come to expect ever-increasing technological conveniences, and we can't imagine living without them. For example, if TV clickers were for some reason banned, many of us would figure that we might as well throw out our television sets.

This brings up the central point of this entire book. This book is about Bible prophecy. It is about our time, a very unique moment in history. A time in which our technology is rapidly changing and in which we're changing as well.

If we can understand these points—that this is a completely unique moment in history, technology is rapidly changing, and we're changing just as quickly—we can begin to understand Bible prophecy in a whole new way.

It's a Different World, Charlie Brown

Think of what television is. We all watch it. But do we have any idea how it works? For most of us the answer is "no, not really." But that doesn't stop us from watching it. Or have you ever looked at one of those huge double-deck airplanes and wondered just how in the world those things fly? But once again, without knowing, we just hop right on them and jet halfway across the world. The same thing is true when we flip on the light switch, start the car, or boot the computer.

For all of us this is no big deal. It's just part of living in the modern age. We go with the flow. But things haven't always been this way. For example, in 1900, Harrods department store in London, England, installed a revolutionary new device. It was called an escalator, and like the ones we ride today, it carried shoppers from the first floor to the second. People didn't know what to think of the new contraption. They worried about what would happen to their bodies if they were to experience such a rapid rise in altitude!

The concerns were so great that Harrods had to comfort those who would use the device by serving them a glass of brandy when they reached the second floor. Now, it wasn't some sales gimmick to advertise the store. It was to help the people getting off the escalator to get over the rapid ascension of twelve feet.

Of course, we know that there were no physical effects that would have come from the rise in altitude. Buildings had had stairs and second floors for centuries. But the people were genuinely scared of the new technology. People then obviously weren't craving the latest invention as we are about a hundred short years later. Indeed, they feared change of any kind while we rush into its waiting arms.

BEEN THERE. DONE THAT. BOUGHT THE T-SHIRT.

So today, what's really amazing isn't just everything that's new, but the way we react to what's new. Nowadays anything new has to be tried and done immediately. What do the commercials say? "Just do it." And what's the complaint of the day? "Been there. Done that."

Do you think a hundred years ago people would have been willing to pay money to tie elastics to their ankles and jump off bridges, almost hitting the ground? We live in a thrill-seeking, instant gratification world. And we just naturally expect things to be better, faster, and newer. The problem, it seems, is that nothing is coming fast enough to satisfy our appetites. In the 1930s when kids read about

Buck Rogers, they wondered if space travel might be possible in their lifetimes or their children's lifetimes. Today when we watch movies about virtual reality, space travel, or artificial intelligence, we wonder if such technology might be possible by Christmas.

TWO. TWO. TWO GENERATIONS IN ONE!

We live at a pivotal moment in history. We live in the single generation that is experiencing the transformation from backwardness to the space age. And it has happened so quickly that we can clearly see, for a brief moment, the two worlds living side by side. For those of us in our middle years, the situation comes clearly into focus as we compare our parents to our children.

Think of the differences in the worlds that our parents lived in and that our children live in today. It's the same planet, but you would hardly think so. The kids speak in the language of megabytes, RAM, VR, cyberspace, and the Net. These words, at the heart of their world, have almost no meaning to just about everyone over fifty today. Grandparents all over the world are complaining that they have no idea what their grandchildren are talking about!

All of this points out something that is totally and completely unique to our day. The technological explosion has created the first true generation gap in human history. In the past kids wore their hair differently from their parents or listened to different music. But today, they truly live in a completely different world. They're plugged in, they're on-line, and they view this world through a lens that the older generation doesn't even know exists. Ah, yes, it is a new world, Charlie Brown.

FOR AN IQ TEST—PRESS CONTROL.ALT.DELETE

We're relatively young men. But we saw the scope of this generation gap not too long ago when we were in a

store here in Niagara Falls looking at some new computers. We're pretty high-tech guys. We have lived around computers for years. As we looked at one of the multimedia systems, two young kids, maybe ten years old, were standing in front of us.
They began to talk about the power of this computer, and we realized that *we* could barely understand what *they* were talking about! Their level of sophistication with

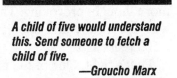

A child of five would understand this. Send someone to fetch a child of five.
            —Groucho Marx

the intricacies of modern microprocessors was staggering. They were ten years old, and we were the ones learning from them. That's happening all over the world for the first time in history. Maybe that's a small part of the reason why they're losing respect for adults. They just think we're clueless.

This Week in Bible Prophecy Ministry has even developed a test that you can use to determine which side of the generation gap you lie on. Go into your family room and take a look at your VCR. If the clock is flashing 12:00, then you're a part of the old world! If that describes you, the next time your child or grandchild comes over, ask her to set your clock. She'll roll her eyes and do it in about twenty seconds.

Finally, we've reached the place in world history that when grandparents tell the "when I was a kid" stories, they truly are describing a very different world from the one in which their grandkids live. Not only are the grandchildren living in a generation that is totally unique from that of their grandparents; they are living in a time that is totally unique from every single generation in history.

By the way, if you were wondering about the subhead to this section, press the control.alt.delete buttons on your keyboard, and you will reboot your computer.

No Way! Are You Serious?

As remarkable as this explosion of knowledge in our generation is, we'd like you to consider something even more thought provoking: This very explosion of knowledge was accurately and specifically prophesied more than 2,500 years ago.

That's right. One of the most overlooked signs the Bible gives concerning the *last days* says that the last generation before the return of Christ would see a great and unique increase in knowledge. In fact, in the prophecy recorded more than 2,500 years ago, an angel told the prophet Daniel that at "the time of the end . . . knowledge shall be increased" (Dan. 12:4).

Now, we know that knowledge has always been on the increase. So what was the angel pointing to that would be specifically unique to the "time of the end"?

If you look at history, every previous generation modestly built on the knowledge gained by the one before it. Thus, each generation was slightly more advanced than the one before it. But the gains were slow. The apostle Paul, for example, sailed in roughly the same type of ships that carried Columbus to the New World 1,500 years later.

Compare that to our day when we've gone from the Wright brothers to the shuttle in well less than a hundred years. That's only one example. All of us could list dozens of examples off the top of our heads because we are a generation, the only generation, that has witnessed an explosive increase in knowledge. That makes this generation different from every other one. In fact, if you're honest, you can't deny that the single most significant description of our generation is exactly that— the birth of the information age.

TIME TUNNEL

Do you remember the old television program that used to be on in the late sixties called *Time Tunnel*? We used to watch that show every week, and then run outside to play with our friends. We'd sit around the crabapple tree in the backyard and imagine what it would be like to have such a device. For those of you who don't have any idea what we're talking about, *Time Tunnel* was about these two guys who had a machine that could transport them through time, into the future, or into the past. In the past, they were able to relive events, like the sinking of the *Titanic*, the fall of Jericho, and the Battle of Waterloo. And in the future they caught a glimpse of where technology was heading.

In one episode, they shot all the way forward to 1978, where the two "chrononauts" (their word, not ours) stowed away on a shuttle to Mars. Though the show may never have been nominated for an Emmy award, the concept was an intriguing one, and as kids we all had different times that we would like to visit. But as kids, we seldom talked about saving the world, or stopping a war before it started. Instead, we wanted to go into the future to see the answers to next week's history test, or into the past to change our answers on last week's history test! For now though, let's talk about the power of such a machine (imaginary though it may be) to help us understand our own generation.

Imagine if you will that you are able to go back in time, pick up a passenger, and then take that lucky person with you for a trip into the future. Let's start by setting the dial on our time tunnel to the year A.D. 800. You find a farmer, working in his field and convince him that it's a good idea to join you for a trip into the future. (Fortunately for you, the shotgun hasn't been invented yet.) Let's start with a short trip, say 100 years. The farmer is staggered by the technology of the day. "Modern" farmers are using a new device called a plow and are tilling twice as much land in half the time. Wow! That's pretty amazing. Back into the tunnel you go, this time emerging 400 years farther into the future, in 1300. Sure there are some new breakthroughs—water mills, better plows, a budding interest in science—but in most parts of the world, there is little to tell that farmer that anything is different. So, here we are, 500 years into the future, and things are looking pretty much the same.

A WHOLE NEW BALL GAME

Now, let's drop that farmer off, back in his time, and take a trip to the 1800s, let's say the 1890s. You find a world filled with wonder, marveling at the incredible advances of the modern, industrial age. Steam engines, automobiles, sewing machines, telephones. This is a pretty amazing world, or so the people living in it seem to think. You grab the first farmer you see (the first one without a shotgun, that is) and talk him into going for a little ride. This time, you take him way into the future, say twenty-five years. On this trip you don't run the risk of having the farmer think you lied to him. You're really in the future now, and the evidence is all around you. Airplanes soar overhead, the Ford factory is cranking out cars at an alarming pace, and a nearby radio is broadcasting the voice of a man fifty miles away. Things that had been declared impossible or that had never even been dreamed of twenty-five years earlier are everywhere!

Next, let's travel with the same guy another twenty-five years into the future, say to 1945. Atomic bombs, aircraft carriers, jet engines, television—you turn around to see what your farmer friend thinks of all this and find him lying flat on his back. Life is moving at a dizzying pace.

Another twenty-five years, and we have men on the moon. Another twenty-five years, and we have the space shuttle, computers, the Internet, satellite TV, and enough nuclear power to blow up the world. And don't just think about where we've come from. Think about where we're going. After having gone from the Wright brothers to the space shuttle in a single lifetime, it's mind-boggling to think of what lies just around the corner.

As one of the foundational descriptions of the last days, it seems pretty clear that we can consider the "increase in knowledge" prophecy to have been right on the mark.

THE START OF SOMETHING BIG

But Bible prophecy is more compelling still. This generation is not just unique from every one that has gone before it; it is also unique from every one that may follow it. That is because you can take the quantum leap from backwardness to the space age only once. It doesn't mean that there couldn't be great increases in knowledge in the future; it just means that you can't have the first quantum leap ever again. That's what makes this generation totally and irreplaceably unique—matching the description of the angel perfectly.

> *Fifteen years from now there will be a microchip in your telephone receiver with more computing power than all the technology the Defense Department can buy today. All the written knowledge in the world will be one of the items to be found in every schoolchild's pocket.*
>
> *—Howard Rheingold, from* Tools for Thought

Consider this: Most experts agree that the sum total of human knowledge, everything we know as a race, is now doubling every two years! This is a staggering statistic. Stated another way, we now know twice as much as we did just two short years ago, and half as much as we will two years down the road.

A recent Gallup poll revealed that 46 percent of Americans felt that they were being left behind by the increases in technological know-how. No kidding! The other 54 percent are probably not being truthful with themselves.

How can you possibly keep up when 80 percent of all the scientists who have ever lived are alive and working today? Or when computer processing power doubles every eighteen months? Or when the total amount of knowledge—everything we've learned from Adam until now—doubles every two years? Yet, somehow, a Hebrew prophet living in Babylon 2,500 years ago foresaw the whole thing.

NASA OR *STAR TREK*?

All of these great breakthroughs and discoveries have had a profound impact on humankind that has gone far beyond the technological realm. They have instilled us with a new level of confidence. We now believe that anything is possible. And with so much going on in so many fields, who can keep track of what is a theory and what has actually been proven or discovered?

Now add into this mixture a heaping portion of science fiction and you have a recipe for massive confusion. In our world today, many people no longer know where the lines between fact and fantasy lie.

Not too long ago, we were with a group of people talking about the advances of modern science. Someone started to tell of the latest research being done on the shuttle. "That's impossible," one of the scientists said. The first person stopped for a moment and then a sheepish grin came upon his face. "Oh. I'm sorry. You're right. I saw that on *Star Trek*!"

With the overwhelming influence of science fiction on television and in the movies, it might even now be said that science will never be able to surprise us again. After all, the images we see in the theaters and in our homes are always ahead of the latest science. So, by the time science catches up, it is old hat. Equally important is the new and unquestioned assumption of our day—that science will ultimately catch up to whatever image we put on the silver screen.

Thus, when we see spacecraft buzzing around in *Independence Day*, or when we re-create dinosaurs from preserved DNA in *Jurassic Park*, the question is not if, but when, science will make such things possible in the real world. And it's no wonder people think this way when we now have our own shuttles flying around out there and test-tube babies are nothing new.

Once again, the key point is that in this generation we've changed as much as the technology has. Our expectations for the future are right off the chart. Nothing is too wild for us to imagine! We want new technologies, we want new thrills, and we want them now. And this raises another almost unimaginable point. Despite the great advances and the "toys" of the day, most of the modern-day world is totally bored. How can this be?

NOW WE WANT SOMETHING, ANYTHING, BIG TO HAPPEN!

We can both remember, as little boys, watching Neil Armstrong step onto the moon. More recently, we remember the first shuttle launch. These have been great times to grow up in. But our imaginations have been fueled by Hollywood far more than they have been by the Johnson Space Center in Houston. In fact, the Smithsonian Institution's *Apollo* display of the actual spacecraft that put man on the moon receives far fewer visitors than the fictional *Star Trek* exhibit! And this points out one of the most significant characteristics of this generation.

E.T., *Star Trek*, and *Independence Day* have painted such powerful images on our collective consciousness that our everyday world and our staggering advancements actually seem a little drab in comparison. Can you believe it? Despite the monumental time in which we live, it's nowhere near enough. Our imaginations have been so stirred by Hollywood that we want, we need, something more. We don't want to watch Arnold Schwarzenegger have all the adventure up on some screen. We want it to happen to us in the real world. When Will Smith, of *The Fresh Prince of Bel-Air*, was saving earth from the aliens in *Independence Day*, the whole world dreamed of an adventure like his.

HOLLYWOOD'S GOT NOTHING ON THIS!

Isn't it amazing that our generation is the very one that so badly wants something "out of this world" to happen? For the student of Bible prophecy, doesn't it seem like a world perfectly set up for the most dramatic event in history—the rapture?

The rapture is the next event on the prophetic calendar, and it is also one of the most dramatic events imaginable. According to the Bible, the generation that saw Israel return to her land, as well as an explosive increase of knowledge, will also see this event—where all Christians, millions and millions of them, suddenly vanish off the face of the earth!

How's that for something big? Any generation before this one would have had a global heart attack at the moment when this happened. But today, the world has been primed. It is looking for something big to happen. To many, the rapture will be the long-awaited beginning of what they hope will be a remarkable adventure.

But let's take it a step farther. Although the Bible

doesn't specifically tell us, it seems likely that when the rapture does take place, the world's first thought may well be that they've been attacked by UFO's. If you think about it, it's the only context people have for seeing someone vanish in front of them. "Beam me up, Scotty," the globally known phrase accompanying the use of *Star Trek*'s transporter beam, has been embedded in the consciousness of millions. Science fiction and New Age thinking have become such an influence on our world that *Star Trek* and its transporter beam will undoubtedly be more readily believed than God. As Sir Francis Bacon wrote, "People prefer to believe what they prefer to be true."

RACING TOWARD . . . WHATEVER

But let's get back to today for a moment. It's as if we live in a world on fast-forward. We're blaring into the future at breakneck speed. Driven by astounding technological breakthroughs and powerful, seductive media images, we have no idea what lies ahead, but we just can't wait to get there!

The danger, of course, is exactly like that involved in barreling down the highway too quickly in your convertible with your hair blowing in the wind. When you're going so fast, there is no time to react to the unexpected or to think about what lies around the next corner.

In today's world, with total knowledge doubling every two years, there is no doubt that the unexpected is about to jump out on the highway in front of us. It just seems that we're hoping that we'll be able to steer clear and not end up in the ditch. However, the faster we go, the more unlikely that is.

THE NINETIES: AS EXCITING AS A SILENT MOVIE

Have you ever looked at the old movies from the turn of the century? You know the ones. They're black and white and everyone is moving at funny speeds. And there is not even any sound.

You know how hard they are to watch. They look so foreign that you can't imagine how people could have lived in such a backward world. Yet they thought they were at the very pinnacle of technological development. One of the most staggering evidences of this belief was something that Charles H. Duell, Commissioner of the U.S. Office of Patents, said in 1899. He surveyed the technologies of the day and concluded that "everything that can be invented has been invented."

Today, we know how ridiculous that is. Yet in some ways we always view our present day as the pinnacle. People thought that way in the twenties, fifties, and seventies.

It is sort of like the bell-bottom-jeans days of the seventies. Man, we thought we were cool in those things. We were hip! We remember trying to get the bell-bottom to cover the entire foot. Today, we look at a TV show from the seventies and have to hide our faces in embarrassment. And suddenly, it seems they're back. It's a good thing our dad never threw his out.

Our point is this. We have studied the issue carefully, and we believe that within ten short years someone looking at the images of our day will see our day as foreign—not as the reruns of *Starsky and Hutch* but as the black-and-white movies of Charlie Chaplin.

Don't forget that if knowledge continues to double every two years, the amount of knowledge we have today will be only one-sixteenth of that possessed in ten years. And computers will be almost 128 times faster and more advanced.

As Seen on TV

As we've pointed out, with so much happening in our world, it's almost impossible to keep up with it all. At the same time much of what we do know about our world and the images that we have of the future comes from a new phenomenon of our day—the mass media.

We all saw the Gulf War. Yet we didn't travel to Kuwait. We saw Nancy Kerrigan skate against Tonya Harding without going to the Olympics, all the while listening to reports from Dave Letterman's mom. And we saw Marcia Clark do battle with Johnnie Cochran in a tiny L.A. courtroom without ever having to leave our living rooms.

If you think about it, TV has become our window on the world. It tells what is happening, what to expect, what to believe, and what to shun. It defines the boundaries of debate, sets the world's focus on some issues while ignoring others. It tells us what is possible and what is real. Yet it is, by its very definition, a medium of illusion and deception. TV doesn't simply show us the world as it is; instead, it is bent and shaped into whatever form the producer chooses.

We believe that in a world in the midst of massive transformation and overwhelmed by information, there is no more powerful weapon than TV. As we saw in the collapse of the entire Communist world, TV is more powerful than armies and more effective than occupying troops. After all, why go to the expense of enslaving people when you can win their hearts?

Amazingly, the Bible told us that the generation that saw this remarkable increase in knowledge would also be swept up in a delusion unlike anything humankind has ever known. Today, for the first time in history we can understand the nature and scope of that deception. We can also see it beginning to unfold.

However, as powerful as television and the silver screen are, both may be about to become obsolete.

DECEPTION? IT'S A VIRTUAL REALITY

Those of you who know our ministry know that we are very careful in what we say. We are generally viewed as being provocative without being sensational. That's because we believe that the world we live in and the fulfillment of the Bible's prophecies that we speak of are sensational enough in and of themselves. They don't need our embellishment.

Having said that, let us say this. The world is about to be rocked by a transformation unlike anything we've ever seen. That's because a new technology lying around the corner is going to literally change everything. We believe that virtual reality is going to have a bigger impact upon this planet than anything since Jesus walked the earth two thousand years ago!

What is virtual reality? Imagine that you're watching a television sitcom—say *Seinfeld*. Now imagine going up to your TV and sticking your head right into it through the screen. In fact, climb right in. Now, instead of watching the program, you are right in the middle of Jerry's living room. You are right in the middle of the action. That's virtual reality.

Imagine putting on a pair of magical glasses that could allow you to become a part of any scene you wanted. You could be walking a Caribbean beach or climbing Mount Everest. That's virtual reality.

You could be at bat in the bottom of the ninth in the deciding game of the World Series. You could be the president of the United States, or you could be a gardener trimming virtual plants in the world's most beautiful virtual garden. That's virtual reality.

YOU'LL NEVER LEAVE THE HOUSE!

Virtual reality refers to computer-generated environments that seem so real that your senses—sight, sound, touch, taste, and even smell—can't tell them from the real world. And such technology is only a few years away.

Consider this Associated Press article from December 18, 1996:

> A desktop computer chip has become the building block of the fastest supercomputer ever built, a machine so powerful it can peer inside human DNA and simulate nuclear explosions . . . "It's a baby step toward being able to do real simulation of the physical world, which is what the Holodeck is all about on 'Star Trek,' " said Justin Rattner, an Intel Supercomputer expert, referring to the virtual reality rooms in the TV series.

Think of what that means. People spend an average of seven hours a day in front of the boob tube. How much time will they spend in a world where they can define every detail exactly to their specifications?

But there is another issue. If you can create every detail of that world, are you not the God of that world? Of course, you are! You can make everyone you create in that world bow down and worship you if you want.

Think of how hard it will be to go back to your assembly line work after being ruler of the universe in your VR system. Here's another prediction of ours. When home VR comes upon the scene, it will be hard to get anyone to even leave the house.

Imagine a world where reality and illusion become so confused. People's senses will literally not be able to tell the virtual world from the real one. *Virtual* used to mean almost as good as the real thing; in a couple of years it will mean it's better.

A WHOLE NEW WAY OF LOOKING AT PROPHECY!

This book is designed for one specific purpose. We want to give you a whole new way of looking at this world and at Bible prophecy.

You see, as we have read the writings of people who sought to understand the prophecies of the Bible many years or centuries before our day, we have been amazed at how clearly they saw the general outline of the final generation. And this is not only a testament to their insights. It is a testimony of how accurate the Bible was in describing our day. After all, centuries ago, men of God could read the prophecies of the Bible and see in faith what we see in reality today.

However, some things were clouded and hidden from them. They could not foresee developments such as worldwide television, computers, or virtual reality. Thus, they could not possibly have had the clear view of prophecy that we have today when we can see these things right before our eyes.

And do you know what? Even this was prophesied in the Bible. Remember that the angel told Daniel that at "the time of the end . . . knowledge shall be increased." Well, that's not all he told the prophet. You see, Daniel was confused by the things he was allowed to see. He tried to describe the things that he was shown in the very best way that he could, but really, he had no idea what was going on.

He asked the angel about this problem, and the angel said something remarkable. He said, "Go thy way, Daniel: for the words are closed up and sealed till the time of the end" (Dan. 12:9). In other words, he was telling Daniel, you can't understand these things; they will make no sense until "the time of the end . . . [when] knowledge shall be increased."

That is why we have to realize that we can see Bible prophecy in a whole new way today. It is the time of the end! Knowledge has been increased! So now these things are beginning to make sense to us.

FOR SUCH AN HOUR AS THIS

We believe that like Esther in the Old Testament, we have indeed been called into the "kingdom for such a time as this" (Est. 4:14). As we've mentioned, we are quite a bit younger than virtually every other major prophetic teacher of this generation.

We are friends with, and have great respect for, virtually every one of them, but our youth allows us to have a slightly different perspective. That's because we have been raised in a very different time.

For example, we were speaking to one well-known prophecy teacher recently, and he shared tremendous insights into the nature of war and rise to power of the Nazis in Germany. They were experiences we could not possibly understand in the way he did. We hadn't even been born yet.

Likewise, we have a particular vantage point to see these new areas of prophetic fulfillment because we live in the midst of the techy, Trekkie, and MTV generation. We use computers every day. We've played all the games. We understand how members of the younger generation are embracing a completely new worldview because they are our generation.

In this book we want to help you understand the unique moment in time in which we live. We want to help you see it through the eyes of that younger generation—a generation ready to accept just about anything. And we want to show you how all of this will completely change and update your understanding of Bible prophecy. If you thought prophecy was amazing before, hold on. You ain't seen nothing yet!

CHAPTER 2

The world is moving so fast these days that the man who says it can't be done is generally interrupted by someone doing it.

—Harry Emerson Fosdick

THE WORLD ON FAST-FORWARD

Let's say you're ten years old, and your brother is slightly older, say twelve. Your father comes up to both of you one afternoon and offers you an intriguing choice. He's going to give you a whole year's allowance up front. That's good news to both of you, and you listen intently to what he says next. You can receive your payment in one of two ways. The first option, which your brother leaps on immediately, is to take a lump sum payment of $1,000. The other option, which you hesitantly decide to accept, is to receive one penny on the first day of January, two pennies on the second day, four on the third, and so on until the end of the month. You don't have a calculator with you, and since we're living in the 1990s you don't even consider figuring it out with pencil and paper. You decide to just wait and see how things work out over the course of the month. Here's a chart showing your payment schedule for the first week of January:

DAY	PAYMENT TO YOU	TOTAL TO YOU SO FAR
Monday, January 1	$0.01	$0.01
Tuesday	$0.02	$0.03
Wednesday	$0.04	$0.07
Thursday	$0.08	$0.15
Friday	$0.16	$0.31
Saturday	$0.32	$0.63
Sunday	$0.64	$1.27

By the end of week one, you're probably starting to wonder if you did the right thing. You look at your brother. He has already bought a new bike, a bunch of comic books, and a computer game, and he still has $700 left. You, on the other hand, count up all your pennies, and you have only a measly $1.27 to your name. Oh well, a deal is a deal. You just hope things are going to get better.

Here's what happens in week two:

DAY	PAYMENT TO YOU	TOTAL TO YOU SO FAR
Monday, January 8	$1.28	$2.55
Tuesday	$2.56	$5.11
Wednesday	$5.12	$10.23
Thursday	$10.24	$20.47
Friday	$20.48	$40.95
Saturday	$40.96	$81.91
Sunday	$81.92	$163.83

Well, things are starting to look a little bit better, but you hope you're not going to run out of month before you catch up. Just to be safe you decide to hold off on putting a down payment on a bike like your brother's. Maybe by the end of next week you'll feel a little more bullish.

DAY	PAYMENT TO YOU	TOTAL TO YOU SO FAR
Monday, January 15	$163.84	$327.67
Tuesday	$327.68	$655.35
Wednesday	$655.36	$1,310.71
Thursday	$1,310.72	$2,621.43
Friday	$2,621.44	$5,242.87
Saturday	$5,242.88	$10,971.51
Sunday	$10,485.76	$20,971.51

Wow! What's going on here? You pick yourself up off the floor as you collect this week's check from Dad. Good thing Dad's a professional basketball player, or he'd have to mortgage the house just to pay your allowance! You laugh at your brother and rush past the bicycle store and right into the motorcycle place. Sure, you're too young to drive it yet, but it'll drive him crazy, and that's worth every penny.

DAY	PAYMENT TO YOU	TOTAL TO YOU SO FAR
Monday, January 22	$20,971.52	$41.943.03
Tuesday	$41,943.04	$83,886.07
Wednesday	$83,886.08	$167,772.15
Thursday	$167,772.16	$335,544.31
Friday	$335,544.32	$671,088.63
Saturday	$671,088.64	$1,342,177.27
Sunday	$1,342,177.28	$2,684,354.55

By the end of the fourth week, the twenty-eighth day of the month, you have learned something valuable. The whole idea of exponential growth and doubling is starting to take on some real meaning. Your brother is now your butler, and your dad has been forced to sign a multiyear deal with his NBA team just to pay your allowance. Only three days left in the month, but who cares? With over $2 million total take so far, who needs those last few days?

DAY	PAYMENT TO YOU	TOTAL TO YOU SO FAR
Monday, January 29	$2,684,354.56	$5,368,709.11
Tuesday	$5,368,709.12	$10,737,418.23
Wednesday	$10,737,418.24	$21,474,836.47

What difference could three days make, you were asking? Well, in the world of exponential growth, those last days are always the biggest. Take a look at the numbers for the last three days. You are going to take home almost ten times as much allowance as you would have if you had made this deal in February, which has only twenty-eight days. You take your $21 million, give your brother your old bicycle, and wonder if you can talk Dad into extending the deal for another week or two.

This little story can go a long way toward making the idea of exponential growth a little easier to understand. More important though, it makes it easier to appreciate. Just look at the rate of growth and how it increases with each passing day. In fact, half of your multimillion-dollar windfall comes on the very last day.

And what does all this have to do with Bible prophecy and the approach of the year 2000? Well, from the book of Daniel we know that one of the key signs of the last days would be an increase in knowledge. And for years now we have known that human knowledge is increasing at an incredible rate. Most scholars agree that the total amount of human knowledge doubled once between 4000 B.C. and the birth of Christ. Then from the birth of Christ to 1750, it doubled again. From 1750 to 1900, it doubled again. From 1900 to 1950, it doubled yet again. Notice how the time frames get shorter and shorter—from 4,000 years to 1,750 years, to 150 years, to 50 years. Then from 1950 to 1960, it doubled again, and now, in this generation, the rate has become exponential, just like our example of the boys and their allowance. The prominent belief now is that the rate of doubling is less than two years.

> *When I turned two I was really anxious, because I'd doubled my age in a year. I thought, if this keeps up, by the time I'm six I'll be ninety.*
> —Steven Wright

Think about that. Every two years, the sum total of all our human knowledge doubles. What a time to be alive! Look at our allowance story again. It's like the month of January was the history of the world, and you just happen to be alive on the thirty-first day. Imagine what marvels must lie just around the corner. Imagine the allowance that you would have collected in the first week of

February. By the end of that week you'd have close to $3 billion! Fasten your seat belt, my friend, and get ready for the future.

<h2 align="center">ONE HUNDRED MILLION BOOKS IN YOUR BRIEFCASE!</h2>

Did you know that scientists have learned more about the world and how it works during your lifetime than in the entire history of the world before you were born? Did you know that if you read just one full issue of the *New York Times* newspaper, you will have absorbed more information than you would have in your entire lifetime had you been born a hundred years ago? Did you know that the Library of Congress now requires more than twenty miles of new bookshelves every year just to accommodate all the new publications?

> *It would appear that we have reached the limits of what it is possible to achieve with computer technology, although one should be careful with such statements, as they tend to sound pretty silly in 5 years.*
> —*John Von Neumann (1949)*

There is no question that we live in a world of information, a world that would have been even more overwhelming than it is if not for the development of new technologies such as computers, CD's, and laser discs. But thanks to these incredible developments, it's now possible to carry around the entire contents of the Library of Congress—in your briefcase. If you're too lazy to carry a briefcase, you can have total access to the library, and almost every scrap of recorded information in the world, by plugging your laptop computer into the nearest telephone jack.

Of course you don't have any hope at all of actually reading all those books, seeing all those movies, watching all those television shows, listening to all those tapes, going to all those lectures, and so on and so on. But computer access does allow us to find what we're looking for, and for most of us, that's about all we need to keep us happy.

So with this incredible deluge of information pouring into our world every day, it's a good thing that one single invention, the microchip, has come along to make our lives a little easier.

1948, THE NEXT GENERATION

Prophecy teachers generally accept that the final countdown to the Lord's return began when the nation of Israel was reborn, on May 14, 1948. Two thousand years ago Jesus used the common biblical symbol of Israel, the fig tree, to demonstrate that the rebirth of this tiny nation would begin the final prophetic countdown:

> Now learn a parable of the fig tree; When his branch is yet tender, and putteth forth leaves, ye know that summer is nigh: so likewise ye, when ye shall see all these things, know that it is near, even at the doors. Verily I say unto you, This generation shall not pass, till all these things be fulfilled. (Matt. 24:32–34)

Well, a lot of things happened in 1948 besides the rebirth of Israel, including the invention of the transistor, perhaps the biggest single technological breakthrough in the history of the world. And so, along with the invention of the transistor, came the birth of a new era, the beginning of the movement from the industrial age to the information age. And when it comes to increases in knowledge and pace of change, you won't find a more vivid example than this thimble-size transistor that sat there on a table in the Bell Telephone Laboratory in New York City for all the world to see.

On that day in 1948, that transistor seemed incredibly small, especially sitting there beside the bulky vacuum tube that it was meant to replace. But that was only the beginning. Within ten years, technicians had placed ten of these transistors on a single silicon wafer, less than one-tenth of an inch square. But even that was nothing. Ten years after that, 10,000 transistors were crowded onto the same tiny square, and for the same price as the ten transistors a decade earlier. Five years later, they had squeezed 16,000 transistors onto that square, and by 1985, 1 million. But it wouldn't stop there. By 1991, there were 16 million transistors on that square. How's that for pace of change? And talk about miniaturization. The smallest transistors today are less than one-seventy-five-thousandth the size of a human hair!

FASTER THAN A SPEEDING BULLET

Helping to feed this incredibly rapid growth in technology is one very important fact. You see, unlike the great technological breakthroughs of the past, the microchip is unique in that it can directly contribute to its own evolution, compounding the rate of change. As faster and faster microchips are developed, they are put to use working on ways to make even faster chips. It's an ongoing process that has obviously led to incredible growth. We should make it clear, however, that not only computers are benefiting from the advances in microchip technology. In reality, almost everything in the developed world has been thrown into fast-forward by this incredible device.

The Internet is a perfect example. With computer technology racing ahead by giant leaps almost every day, things such as the Internet are suddenly jumping from almost total obscurity to worldwide predominance in a very short period of time.

And is the trend likely to continue? A well-known

axiom in the computer industry has become known as Moore's law, named for Gordon Moore, the founder of the world's largest microchip manufacturer, Intel. According to Moore's law, the total amount of information that can be stored on a single silicon chip doubles every eighteen months, while during that same time, the cost of making the chips falls by 50 percent. This law has managed to stay valid for more than twenty years since Moore first postulated it back in the mid-seventies. The performance of microprocessors has improved more than 25,000 times in the last twenty years.

Although not everyone agrees about how long Moore's law can continue to hold up, most agree that it will stay in effect for at least another decade. And remember, doubling the amount of storage on a chip means doubling the power of computers. Certainly, for the immediate future, the rapid pace of change is going to continue, and within ten to fifteen years, *one* computer will be as powerful as *all* of the computers in the world today.

As other technologies race forward to complement the microchip, the entire world is being thrown into fast-forward. Among the most dramatic examples is the rapid increase in the amount of information that can be sent across town or around the world through fiber-optic cable.

> *Change is inevitable—except from a vending machine.*
> *—Robert C. Gallagher*

A new information transmission speed record was recently set in New York, where researchers succeeded for the first time in transmitting information at a rate of 1 trillion (1,000,000,000,000) bits per second. To give this feat some perspective, consider that we are talking about the equivalent of more than three hundred years' worth of large daily newspapers being transmitted in a single second.

In terms of voice communications, we are talking about the ability to carry 12 million telephone conversations simultaneously through a tiny glass wire smaller than a human hair. For several years, this transmission capacity (1 trillion bits per second) has been considered the "Holy Grail" of the electronic communications world, and today, it has become a reality. Adding to the incredible feat that this already is, is the fact that the previous transmission speed record was a mere 400 billion bits per second, achieved only a year earlier. How's that for rapid advancement?

THEY'RE EVERYWHERE! THEY'RE EVERYWHERE!

Even more important to our generation than the size and speed of computers is what we are using them for. And that has been expanding almost as quickly. In 1972, there were only about 150,000 computers in the world. Compare that to today. Intel, the world's largest chip manufacturer, is planning to ship nearly 100 million computer processors this year. In the United States alone, shipments of computers within the country have risen from 53,000 in 1976 to almost 19 million in 1996.

When we're talking about the explosion of the computer age, we're not only talking about the PC's that sit on desktops around the country. The computer revolution has moved well beyond that, making computers an important part of almost every life in America. Even the die-hard traditionalists, who claim to prefer the old-fashioned way of writing letters, doing taxes, and playing solitaire, use computers throughout the day without ever even realizing it. It's almost impossible to get through a day without using computers in one way or another. Whether you're adjusting the thermostat on your living room wall, buying a quart of milk at the supermarket checkout, or checking the messages on your answering machine, chances are, you're using a computer. Even when you're driving your car down the road, you're surrounded by computer technology. An incredible 83 percent of a new car's functions from fuel injection to power brakes are controlled by microprocessors. Four years ago, the figure was 18 percent.

As for PC's that are becoming more and more common in homes around the world, that trend is likely to continue in much the same way the trend for color televisions did a generation ago. But this time, it's likely to move even more quickly. Consider that in 1960, fewer than 1 percent of American families had a color television set. Today, 98 percent of homes have at least one color TV, and most have two or more. Why was there such incredible market penetration for these devices? They became affordable, and

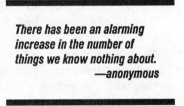

There has been an alarming increase in the number of things we know nothing about.
—anonymous

in the eyes of the buying public anyway, they became an *essential part* of life. Computers are already getting to the point that they don't cost very much more than color TV sets, and probably by the year 2000, computers, complete with Internet connections, will be as commonplace as televisions are today.

It's really hard to predict, however, just how quickly computers are going to continue to move into our lives. But as you think about it, think about IBM's boast in 1980 that the world market for computers in the coming decade could reach as high as 275,000. Was the estimate close? Not really. The actual number was more than 60 million.

MORE FOR LESS

Obviously, as we have discussed, one basic factor in this incredible increase has been affordability. Even ten years ago, computers were far too expensive for the average person to consider owning. When our ministry first entered the computer age, back in about 1987, we had to pay close to $10,000 for a computer that is laughable today. Chances are pretty good that the watch you're wearing right now has more processing power than that computer did. Oh, well, it did the job, and most important, we had nothing to compare it to. This is actually one of the keys to satisfaction in the world of technology. Today, a computer one thousand times faster and with five hundred times more storage capacity costs less than $1,500! To put the whole cost factor into perspective, consider this: If computer memory cost the same today as it did in 1960, an average PC today would cost more than $30 million.

The final element that is of tremendous significance to the information age is ease of use. Not long ago, computers were the exclusive domain of what were then known as eggheads. They were the prototypical computer geeks, with the plastic pocket protectors, the thick glasses with the tape in the middle, and pants that didn't quite make it all the way down to the ankles. Today, computers sit on almost every desktop in the country, and in nearly half of American homes. And like everything in the computer world, these statistics are also on the increase. Obviously, a big part of this phenomenon is the fact that even though computers are getting more and more powerful, they are getting easier to use at the same time. Children who aren't even old enough to go to school are clicking and surfing their way through the wonderful world of cyberspace. For millions of kids, computers have already become toys. Nintendo, one of the world's largest manufacturers of computer games, has now developed a computerized video game that will cost about $250. This game will offer kids the same computing power that cost $14 million only ten years ago.

THE ILLUSION OF SPACE AND TIME

As incredible as much of the progress we have seen in the computer age is, we need to note something else. A lot of the gains are enhanced even further by something of an illusion. You see, advances in compression technology allow many of these breakthroughs to appear even greater than they are.

In terms of storage space on computers, for example, compression technologies developed in the past couple of years have literally allowed people to radically expand the size of their computer hard drives without having to replace any hardware. By using software that compresses information on the fly, you can now fit a two-hundred-page book into the same amount of computer storage space that used to hold only fifty pages. And because the software does its work "behind the scenes," the user isn't even aware of what is

A computer lets you make more mistakes faster than any invention in human history— with the possible exceptions of handguns and tequila.
—*Mitch Ratliffe*

happening. What is the end result of all of this? Suddenly, overnight, with the click of a button, computers around the world hold two or three times as much as they did yesterday.

This same illusion is carried over into the area of time as well. By moving compressed files instead of fully expanded ones, we *seem* to be able to move information that much more quickly too. Again, the actual breakthroughs are great, but advances in computer technology have made them appear even greater than they really are.

These developments can be a lesson to anyone trying to understand what life might be like in the future. The lesson is simple—our ability to predict what lies just around the corner is often constrained by barriers that may seem very solid today. Five years ago, when people were trying to imagine sending digital images such as movies and television pictures through the Internet, they seemed to be faced with an impossible obstacle. How do you get all that data through a phone line? Today, of course, the answer is clear: Simply compress the data, send it through, and decompress it at the other end. What had seemed impossible is now possible, thanks to a breakthrough that no one was even thinking about.

DANGER: Fast-Pace Zone Ahead

Clearly, there is often an element of danger when things move as quickly as they have in this century, and as they will continue to do in the days ahead. We have seen this many times in our history, especially in our recent history. A notable example is the X-ray machine. Although X rays can be a very useful tool, we also know that they can be extremely dangerous because they expose us to potentially deadly radiation every time they're used.

For that reason, they are used under very specific conditions, and you've probably noticed that doctors and nurses hide behind lead shields or leave the room altogether when the X-ray machine is being used. But when X rays were first discovered, no one had any idea that they were so dangerous. After all, the deadly radiation was completely invisible, and having an X ray taken was certainly not a painful experience. So, with no reason to think anything was wrong with it, shoe stores started installing the machines as something of a marketing gimmick. For years, you could go into shoe stores around the world and look at the bones of your feet inside the new shoes. As little children laughed with delight and wiggled their toes, their parents stood by enjoying the scene, not knowing that their kids were being exposed to deadly radiation.

Another horrible example, etched in the minds of parents around the world, is the drug thalidomide, given to millions of pregnant women in the 1950s and 1960s to help control their morning sickness. What wasn't known at the time was that the drug would have terrible effects on nearly ten thousand children, who were born with flippers instead of arms and legs. Although banned for use in most of the world, it is still used regularly in some countries, and according to a report by the television program *60 Minutes*, thalidomide babies are still being born in Brazil almost every day. This tragedy highlights not only the dangers of our fast-paced world, but also the dangers of a world that is slow to react when the dangers are discovered and the "cure" is inconvenient or expensive.

At one time, smoking tobacco was considered totally harmless, and millions of people ended up developing a deadly addiction to this killer drug. Today, it is a clear medical and scientific fact that smoking can and does kill people every single day. But powerful tobacco companies and millions of addicted smokers have made it all but impossible for anything to be done about it. As a result, millions of lives are lost and billions of dollars are spent, caring for the victims of this drug, once thought to be completely harmless.

Today, we are in real danger of stories like these becoming very commonplace and much, much more severe. Why? You'd think that with all of our scientific sophistication, we'd be better able to weed out the dangerous new technologies. Besides, aren't there a lot more laws and government regulations in place to make sure that something like the thalidomide tragedy doesn't happen again? The answer to that, fortunately, is yes. Drugs must be studied much more carefully before they come to market, and in the age of the lawsuit, companies are a lot more cautious about what products they introduce. Remember, this is the world where a woman successfully sued McDonald's for serving coffee too hot when she spilled it on her lap and burned her leg.

But the real danger for the future comes from the fact that we are really starting to "play with the big pieces" in many areas of science and technology. Experimentation and development in areas such as nuclear power, genetic engineering, and biotechnology mean that when something does go wrong, the results can be absolutely disastrous. And in a world blazing down the highway at top speed, the damage can be done before we even know it. As Nathaniel Borenstein says, in the computer age, "the most likely way for the world to be destroyed, most experts agree, is by accident. That's where we come in; we're computer professionals. We cause accidents."

THIRTY MILES PER HOUR? IMPOSSIBLE!

In spite of the obvious dangers of our rapid pace of change, for the most part, we want three things from technology: more, more, and more! And that makes our generation unique from all the others that have gone before. When the Wright brothers took their historic first flight at Kitty Hawk in 1903, most of the press didn't even cover it. And even when they did manage to get their "flying machine" off the ground, few were very impressed. Octave Chanute, a famous engineer of the day, peered into the future and determined that "such flying machines may even carry mail in special cases, but the useful loads carried will be very small. The machines will eventually be fast, they will be used in sport, but they are not to be thought of as commercial carriers."

Likewise, when railroads were really starting to build momentum late in the last century, the world was less than enthusiastic, and many people were more than a little apprehensive. One California newspaper worried that "the huge iron rails will reverse the Earth's magnetic field with catastrophic effects." As for the future of the railway, there was a problem with the speed at which the trains were able to travel. The Royal Society in England warned against the railways, saying that at speeds over thirty miles per hour, the air supply would be cut off, and anyone riding on the train would die of asphyxiation. Jumping onto the bandwagon, the College of Physicians in Munich, Germany, added that at speeds like that (thirty miles per hour), passengers would suffer headaches, vertigo, and possibly the loss of their sight. But most agreed that the passenger problem would never have a chance to be tested, because at speeds approaching thirty miles per hour, even a tiny twig would shatter the huge metal wheels.

Compare that attitude with what we see in the world today. We are so much the opposite that these illustrations seem ridiculous. Rather than fearing technology and doubting that major breakthroughs are possible, we are demanding more and more, and believing that nothing is impossible. We've become a generation of spoiled brats, demanding *and expecting* more from technology and less from ourselves every day.

GET
READY

_____
_____
_____
_____
_____
_____
_____
_____
_____
_____
_____
_____
_____
_____
_____
_____

The most characteristic thing about mental life, over and beyond the fact that one apprehends the events of the world around one, is that one constantly goes beyond the information given.

—Jerome Bruner

THE ADVENTURES OF THE INDIANA LALONDES

(KEEPING UP WITH THE JONESES)

It was a hot summer night in North Bay, Ontario, Canada, in 1976. We were two teenage boys, minding our own business, walking home from the movie theater, taking, as we often did, a shortcut along the beach. The movie we had just seen had both of us very excited. It was *Raiders of the Lost Ark*, the story of Indiana Jones and his incredible supernatural adventures as he explored the Middle East in search of the ark of the covenant. Like every other person leaving that theater, we were still pumped, grabbing pieces of rope and cracking them like whips. In the same way that kids leaving a good karate movie tend to kick over every garbage can in their path, we were ready to explore every secret passageway we might encounter. Of course in the middle of North Bay, there weren't unexplored pyramids or ancient ruins, so we had to rely largely on the richness of our imaginations. But then, our dreams were realized. We were standing face-to-face with our very own "mystery from beyond."

When we first saw that light reflecting on the surface of

the still lake waters, we were ready for action. "Whips" in hand, we carefully walked up and down the beach in front of the mysterious light, studying it as carefully as we could. What could it be? A UFO? A mysterious signal from another dimension? Maybe even a message from God? One thing was certain, it was no ordinary light. It had no source. Even though the reflection was there, as clear as could be, there was no other light in sight. No moon, no street lamp, not even an unusually bright star. Being rational young men, we immediately ruled out UFO's and mysterious signals from another dimension. Obviously, it had to be a message from God.

What happened next varies depending upon who is telling the story, but we were bound and determined to explore further. As if being drawn by some mysterious force, we both waded out into the water, fully dressed, poorly armed, and more than a little scared. We walked slowly, alternately looking at the light on the water and the empty night sky above. What could it be?

But the plot thickened as we moved closer to the light and saw, inexplicably, that the light itself was moving slowly . . . back and forth . . . back and forth. One of us reached out with a very tentative toe and tried to see if the light would shine through onto a soaking wet sneaker. It was then that the light started spinning, waking us as if from a bad dream. What a disappointment! Our great mystery of the universe was a cheap plastic flashlight, lying in the sand in four feet of water, right where a cat burglar had tossed it a few minutes before. Talk about a letdown. Suddenly, as we stood there on the beach, our clothes dripping, we felt not so much like action heroes as total idiots. Rather than burst through the front door of the house with news of a great discovery, we slid quietly in through the back and, until now anyway, kept the little adventure to ourselves.

And why, you might ask, have we now decided to relive the experience and to share it with millions of readers?

Well, for a couple of reasons. For one, it's a true story. It really happened. But more important, it illustrates several of the most important characteristics of our generation and how those characteristics will play a key role in the last days deception prophesied in the Bible.

Finally, we'd like to make one more observation. When we first saw that light, dancing on the surface of the lake, we decided it must be a message from God. Later, we found out it was only a flashlight. Today, it is clear that it was both! It may have taken us more than twenty years to figure it out, but today, as we write these words, we know that there was an important message lying in four feet of water that night. We hope you'll be able to learn something from our little experience too, and you won't even have to get wet in the process.

I GUESS YOU HAD TO BE THERE

Probably the most powerful aspect of our situation that evening, as we walked home along the beach, is also the most obvious. And that characteristic is probably best summed up by one word—*context*. *Webster's Dictionary* defines *context* as "the whole situation, background or environment relevant to a particular event," and our story really doesn't make very much sense without it. We've probably all had the experience of sharing a story that we thought was incredibly funny and then being greeted by a blank stare, or maybe a polite smile if we're lucky. What is our answer to that reaction? "I guess you had to be there." Obviously, we believe that if they had been there, *sharing the whole context*, they would be able to understand the humor the same way we do. What if our little story included the part about finding the flashlight, but not the part about its happening on the way home from watching *Raiders of the Lost Ark*? You'd probably have wondered, "What's the matter with these guys?" Without the context, or framework, the story doesn't seem to make much sense. (We're hoping, of course, that within the framework, it *does* actually make sense.)

But the fact remains that we were on the way home from a big-screen, Indiana Jones adventure. We had just seen a movie not only brilliantly produced, but absolutely chock-full of excitement, intrigue, and supernatural events too. If some guys had thrown that flashlight into the water, just to see if they could get someone to wade in fully dressed, they couldn't have picked a better time. What, for example, would have happened if we had been on our way home from watching a baseball game that night? That's hard to say for sure, but it's unlikely that we would have gone home soaking wet.

Let's consider an even more dramatic example. What if we had been returning from the theater, but instead of seeing *Raiders of the Lost Ark*, we had just seen the movie *Jaws*? Wow! You want to talk about context. It's probably pretty safe to say that you wouldn't have gotten either of us to wade out into that water for anything. But remember, the situation on that beach would have been physically identical. The light would have looked exactly the same. But the context would have been totally different. Specifically, instead of expecting a message from God, we'd have expected to be eaten by a great white shark, even though that is fairly unlikely in five feet of fresh water. What a difference context can make!

But you don't need to watch a multimillion-dollar action adventure movie to dramatically affect the element of context. Consider another example. Imagine, if you will, the sound of footsteps on the sidewalk behind you. Would that same sound have a different meaning on a Saturday afternoon from what it would on a darkened street in the middle of the night? You better believe it would! And yet, when you think about it, as far as the actual sound is concerned, it is identical in both cases. But because the context is radically different, the two situations are completely different too, and so are your reactions.

So, just as *Raiders of the Lost Ark* powerfully affected our context that night, our entire generation is being influenced by powerful new images, visions, and possibilities. Seeing clear, perfect images on the big screen or on the TV sets in our homes has made us a generation ready for anything. Every day new ideas are powerfully etched into our minds and into our consciousness.

GREAT EXPECTATIONS!

That summer night, we were walking home from the movie in a state of absolute anticipation, believing that some kind of an adventure could be, or even *would* be, waiting for us around the very next corner. And we all know that if we're looking hard enough for something, very often we'll find it, or at least we'll think we find it.

Some years ago, our cousin and a few of her friends decided to do something that was fairly common among young teenagers at the time. They decided to hold a séance. In their young minds, this was not a demonic activity, but just another party game, with no more negative effects than a game of scrabble.

Since Martin Luther King, Jr., had just been shot, they decided to try to contact his spirit. They dimmed the lights, lit some candles, and went through whatever procedures they felt were appropriate for such an event.

After a few minutes, as they all sat around that table, something happened. A spider dropped from the ceiling right in front of them and hung over the middle of the table. You can probably guess what happened next. Every one of them ran up the stairs screaming, scared to death by what they thought they had encountered. They thought

Martin Luther King had come back to life, in the form of a spider, and scared the daylights out of all of them.

Like all of our stories, this one is absolutely true, and we hope that like all of our stories, it also illustrates an important point. Those girls thought that spider was a ghost of Dr. King because that's what they had been looking for. They desperately wanted something to happen, and so, sure enough, it did. Their anticipation was so great that when that spider appeared, their brains went into autopilot assuming that what they were seeing was what they were expecting.

Today, the world is living in a state of absolute expectancy, truly believing that our world is in for some kind of a major transformation that will change the very foundations of life as we know it. Why? Well, there are a lot of reasons, including the powerful images of Hollywood. But certainly, the pace of change in the world has a lot to do with it too. After all, we have seen humankind go from the Wright brothers' first flight at Kitty Hawk to a man walking on the moon in only sixty years! So as we sit here today, watching the space shuttle carrying humans into space like a giant Greyhound bus, we have to ask the obvious question. Where do we go from here? From the Wright brothers to the space shuttle and then from the space shuttle to what? Suddenly, it's as if the whole world is living in that same state of expectancy that we were in that night.

We want to believe that something more is out there. For some, it's a search for their psychic powers, long hidden in that mysterious untapped portion of the brain. For others, it's the emerging belief that we're all one, every molecule in the universe somehow unified by an as-yet-undiscovered mystical connection. For still others, it's the anticipation of contact from an alien species, letting us know for certain that we are not alone in the universe. Whatever it may be, the theme remains the same. Ours is a generation not only ready for something big, but also anxiously anticipating it or even pursuing it with vigor and determination.

That night, as we stood in the water, we were in a mind-set of total expectancy. When we saw that light on the water, we didn't immediately assess the possible logical explanations. We thought we were finding what we were hoping to find. That is the power of expectancy.

GOT WHAT I ASKED FOR

Just as our expectation that an "Indiana Jones" adventure awaited us on the way home from the movie caused us to actually "find" an adventure, so too will people find their "adventure" if they want it badly enough. And this whole idea of great expectations really underscores much of what this generation is all about. More so than at any time in the past, ours is a world filled with anticipation, reaching out for, and often finding, things that we cannot explain. And this yearning is not limited to one particular social or economic group. Instead, it cuts across the whole of society, touching almost all of us in one way or another.

Take Hillary Clinton, for example. Here is a well-educated woman, a lawyer, the first lady of the most powerful nation on the planet, conducting séances and trying to contact the spirits of dead people. Publicly, she considers herself a "committed Christian" and a "serious, reflective and prayerful woman," but on weekends she likes to chat with Mahatma Gandhi, and Eleanor Roosevelt. Mrs. Clinton can take some solace, however, in the fact that she is far from alone. Nancy Reagan used astrologers, whom she believed could help guide the nation. Studies showed New Age philosophy to be of "significant interest" to about 500,000 Americans in 1976, but a follow-up investigation in 1996 showed that the number had swelled to more than 20 million! It's a sign of the times.

HAS ONE IN THREE AMERICANS GONE BONKERS?

So what do all of these people seem to have in common? Their sense of expectancy. Their absolute belief that something big is due to happen, and that this is the generation that is going to see it. Whether it's contact with aliens from another planet, dead humans from another time, or spirits from another dimension, this generation has left every door wide open, and its members are ready for something sensational. A recent *Time*/CNN poll has shown that one in three American adults actually expects that we'll be contacted by aliens in the next one hundred years. Think about that. One in three. If you're in a room with two other people right now, ask around. You might be surprised at what you hear.

REALITY? ZZZ . . .

Another implication of living in a world of unbelievable knowledge and rapid pace of change is the fact that we're becoming increasingly difficult to impress. Even if something does come along that does manage to impress us, we don't stay that way for very long. Part of this situation is certainly brought about by the continuous flood of new technologies into our lives. But the media play a big role too. Every movie seems to push things a little farther, making it harder and harder for the reality of our everyday lives to compete. And on television, we're constantly assailed with images that make reality seem more than a little dull. That was the world we were tasting on our way home from the movie that night. Our lives sure did seem boring and devoid of higher purpose compared to the adventures of Indiana Jones.

We've all heard the expression "been there, done that." That is almost an anthem of the young people of this generation. For kids growing up today, in a world of computers, the Internet, space travel, and satellite dishes, it doesn't take them very long to get bored with what they have, and start looking for the next step. Even though they're working (or playing) on computers that are hundreds of times faster than the fastest computers five years ago, they still aren't happy and want something just a little faster. TV screens keep getting bigger, cars keep getting faster, and our tolerance for the status quo is disappearing.

IMAGINATION, THOU ART LOOSED!

A few short years before the Wright brothers launched their first successful airplane flight at Kitty Hawk, Lord Kelvin declared that "heavier than air flying machines are impossible." And he wasn't alone. Many people considered the whole idea to be complete quackery, and even the press showed very little interest in their little "experiments." Similarly, Napoleon, commenting on Fulton's plans for a steamship, said, "You would make a ship sail against the winds and currents by lighting a bonfire under her deck. . . . I have no time for such nonsense." And to be sure, those people had reason to be skeptical. They were new and radical ideas in times when new and radical developments were much fewer and farther between than they are today.

But today, if you start asking around, there are very few things that people are willing to go on record describing as impossible. That's completely unique to this generation. Traveling faster than the speed of light, transporting people on a beam of light, building cities on other planets—none of it seems out of the question anymore. Things that not long ago were considered pure science fiction are today merely futuristic. The wonderful things that we see on *Star Trek* are no longer thought of as fantasy. Instead, the show gives us a look at what our world will be like in a few short years.

Actually, there are also times when the distinctions between fact and fantasy are obscured in the present day. Movies and television have the power to change our fundamental belief systems, to make us believe that things that are impossible are possible. In our particular story, the movie did exactly that to us. It fueled our imaginations and, at least temporarily, loosened our tight reins on what we believed was possible and what was not.

THE SHARK IN THE SWIMMING POOL

Imagine that you're standing on a street corner with a crowd of other people around eleven o'clock at night and you see a light flash across the sky. Was it a falling star? A meteorite? An airplane crashing? A UFO? Do you think you might make different judgments if you had just finished watching a movie such as *Star Wars* or *Independence Day* than if you had just come out of the planetarium? It's very likely that you would.

What about the movie *Jaws*? Did you know people who were actually afraid to go into the water for a while after seeing that movie? And who could blame them? That *was* a very scary movie. But what is really amazing is that the effect wasn't limited to the areas where sharks are usually sighted. People were afraid to swim in freshwater lakes and even swimming pools. By combining vivid imagery with powerful music and strong emotion, movie producers seem to be able to change our perceptions of what is real and what is possible.

Another example is the movie *Jurassic Park*. In that movie, scientists find tiny fragments of DNA, entombed in amber, that have somehow been perfectly preserved for millions of years. DNA is the genetic material found in every living thing that contains the blueprint or instructions for creating that life-form. By extracting those DNA samples and carefully growing them through very exacting scientific procedures, the scientists in the movie were able to create living, breathing dinosaurs. It made for great science fiction, that much is certain. But it did something else too. You see, we talked to many people who had seen the movie and asked them a few questions, just to see what they were thinking. Those conversations shocked us. Most of the people expressed a sincere wish that such perfectly preserved DNA fragments actually existed. That way, those exacting scientific procedures could be put to task, and real dinosaurs could be produced. They actually thought that the missing element was the DNA, not the technology to turn that DNA into living creatures.

So remember, belief is a subjective thing, and it's important not to allow your brain to run on autopilot. If you hear something that seems a little radical, question it, investigate it, find out for yourself if it's something that you're willing to believe. Of course, you don't have time to do that with everything you come across, and frankly, there is no real need. There is no need to understand how a telephone works in order to make a call. But stand guard at the door of your mind when it comes to new beliefs— because once you start believing something to be true, it can be very hard to change your mind.

WHAT A GENERATION TO BE LIVING IN

So often, when we hear about the last days, we hear about earthquakes, famines, and wars. And to be sure, these and other events are the signs that the Bible gives us to identify the times in which we are living. Moreover, while much of what makes this generation unique is not specifically mentioned in the Bible, on closer examination we see that many of these characteristics are very definitely key components of the last days scenario. So key that understanding them can really help bring Bible prophecy to life.

As we have discussed, we are a generation with a very special context, a very special worldview, created by a combination of factors that didn't exist in any other generation. Today, we have worldwide television. We've entered the space age and the computer generation. Knowledge is doubling every two years. And Hollywood movies are beaming powerful images into our hearts and into our minds. We have an insatiable appetite for new and wonderful breakthroughs. We're unwilling to declare anything impossible anymore, maintaining a fundamental core belief that whatever we can create in our minds, we can create in reality. And what is most important as we think back on the things we've been talking about is that all of these factors are coming into play at exactly the same time.

You see, when these factors add together, they do so with explosive results. Combining any two of these factors does not make the effect twice as strong. Far from it. In reality, the whole effect is much more than the sum of its parts. Like adding nitro and glycerin, the results can be explosive.

*The deliberate creation of unreality is one of the most pivotal social forces shaping our time.*
—Ian Mitroff and Warren Bennis, Thesis of the book The Unreality Industry

THE GOSPEL OF
STAR TREK

So you're telling me that at any minute now, millions of people are going to just simply vanish off the planet, and the Bible predicted it thousands of years ago?"

"That's right. It's called the rapture."

"What happens then?"

"Well, for those who have vanished they get to be with Jesus forever. But for the rest of the world, it marks the beginning of a seven-year time of deception called the Tribulation."

"Okay, here's the deal. If millions of people vanish, and it turns out that they are indeed all you crazy Christians, then I'll believe it."

"I wish it were that easy. But there are going to be compelling reasons to believe that it wasn't the rapture. You can't even begin to imagine how convincing the other gospel is going to be."

"The other gospel! What other gospel?"

"The gospel of *Star Trek*."

HEY, THAT GUY JUST SWITCHED BRIEFCASES!

If you've ever watched any spy movies, you've probably seen it. It's the famous briefcase-switch scene. The bad guy casually walks up to the good guy who is sitting in a chair or standing at a telephone booth. When no one is looking, he carefully leans down and places his counterfeit briefcase next to the original. Then bam! The original is gone, and all that is left is the clever impostor.

That is exactly what the Bible tells us is going to happen in the last days. God is going to allow Satan to bring forth his false christ (the Antichrist) and his own false gospel as well.

Now, for this counterfeit gospel to deceive the whole world, it is going to have to be doubly clever. Think about it for a moment. Not only will it have to provide humankind with a powerful alternative belief system, but it will also have to be able to explain away the events that God has said will happen. In other words, it will have to provide a false explanation for the rapture and the signs and wonders that the Antichrist and his cohorts will be able to perform during the Tribulation period.

We should consider something else. If we are living in the last moments before the rapture, it makes sense that we should be seeing the emergence of that other gospel in the world today.

TO BOLDLY GO

That is exactly what's happening, as if on cue. And this counterfeit gospel is diverse and far-reaching. It is coming at the world from so many different angles that it would take an entire book just to list them all. But all of its strands are pretty well represented in one place, television's *Star Trek*.

That's right. In the continuing adventures aboard the good ship *Enterprise*, there is an entire belief system so complete, so compelling, and so powerful that it literally represents the greatest alternative to the gospel that has ever been offered to mankind. And given the sense of expectancy and anticipation that exists in our world today, it is a counterfeit tailored perfectly for this exact moment in history.

Did you know that when *Star Trek* first appeared on TV in the 1960s, it wasn't well received at all? It may surprise you to hear that the program never even cracked NBC's top-fifty charts.

So how could a program that was barely able to keep itself on the air three decades ago now have such an incredible impact in our day? Simple. As humankind began to see the *Apollo* space programs and the birth of the space shuttle, it became more and more in tune with the ideas of exploring the universe. *Star Trek* went into syndication and became one of the most popular television series of all time. The enthusiasm was so great that the show's producer, Gene Roddenberry, decided to move into the movie business, launching his first feature film, *Star Trek—The Motion Picture*.

Since then, several *Star Trek* movies have followed, and each was a phenomenal success. *Star Trek Generations*, released in 1994, for example, grossed almost $100 million at the box office, further reinforcing the impact of *Star Trek* in this generation.

SPACE, THE GREAT BLACK HOPE

To best understand the counterfeit gospel represented by *Star Trek*, we need to first look at the true gospel. The Greek word that is translated as "gospel" could just as easily be translated as the "good news." And that's what it is, the good news of Jesus Christ. However, this good news comes with a price. Acceptance of the gospel carries with it a responsibility to the One who created us. And that has never sat well with most of humankind.

So, any alternative gospel will need to have its own version of good news. And wouldn't it be more acceptable if it came without the baggage? No need for repentance, no need to deal with sin, just peace and happiness on our own terms. After all, what future sounds more promising: one in which our sins are judged or one in which we just cruise the universe in search of new life-forms and exciting adventures? For the unsaved, the choice is clear.

That is the power of *Star Trek*. People like the picture that it paints of the future better than God's plan. In the *Star Trek* future, human worldly problems have been solved, and generally, everyone seems to get along very well. Members of the human race seem to have worked out their differences and are now working toward the common goal of "seeking out new life and new civilizations."

> *Nothing puzzles me more than time and space, and yet nothing puzzles me less, for I never think about them.*
> —*Charles Lamb*

But that's not all. You see, there are many *species* of creatures from other planets too. Klingons, Cardassians, Ferengis, and dozens of other odd-looking beings are out there in the United Federation of Planets.

Surely, this seems like a noble and desirable outcome, and it suggests to the viewer that there is hope for humankind after all. But most important, this picture gives the non-Christian world something to hang on to and something to believe in. It helps them to believe that maybe there is hope for this increasingly violent, polluted, and corrupt world. By keeping their focus on *Star Trek*, they can confidently say, "Sure, I can imagine a future where all of our problems have worked themselves out."

That's just what *Star Trek* provides, an alternative vision of the future.

And the appeal is nearly universal. It has the potential to touch everyone who has ever stared up into the sky on a clear summer night and wondered what it would be like to travel to the stars. And there is probably not a person alive today who hasn't done that at one time or another.

THE PREPARATION FOR DELUSION

Earlier we mentioned that this counterfeit gospel must achieve two ends. First, it must provide an alternative message of good news to the world. We've seen how the vision represented in *Star Trek* does just that. Remember, we're not just talking about *Star Trek* here. It is just one convenient representation of a new belief system, a new vision that is sweeping the planet.

But we've also noted how any counterfeit gospel, if it was to stand up in the last days, would have to provide an alternative explanation for the things that God said were going to happen during that time.

The perfect example is that of the rapture. The Bible tells us that before the Antichrist rises onto the world scene, millions of people are going to literally vanish off the face of the earth:

> For this we say unto you by the word of the Lord, that we which are alive and remain unto the coming of the Lord shall not prevent them which are asleep. For the Lord himself shall descend from heaven with a shout, with the voice of the archangel, and with the trump of God: and the dead in Christ shall rise first: Then we which are alive and remain shall be caught up together with them in the clouds to meet the Lord in the air: and so shall we ever be with the Lord. (1 Thess. 4:15–17)

According to the Bible, those people will be the believers who are alive at that time. They won't have to die. They will be straight on their way to heaven. So how could a counterfeit gospel deal with this remarkable event?

BEAM ME UP, SCOTTY

If the rapture had happened one hundred years ago, there would have been absolutely no context within which those who were left behind would be able to make sense of what had happened. The same could be said of every other generation. Every other generation, that is, but this one!

A story that has been around for years tells of a young man who had a little too much to drink and managed somehow to run his car through a red light and into a police car parked by the side of the road. Finding himself in a position that was more than a little difficult to defend, he stood before the judge in a crowded courtroom and waited to enter his plea. When the judge turned to him and asked him if he had anything to say, he took out his wallet, flipped it open, and said in a loud, clear voice, "Beam me up, Scotty."

There is a maxim about the universe which I always tell my students: That which is not explicitly forbidden is guaranteed to occur.
—Lawrence M. Krauss,
The Physics of Star Trek

Whether or not the events actually took place is unimportant. The story illustrates the impact that the images of *Star Trek* are having upon our world.

Ask around and try to find someone who has never heard the expression "Beam me up, Scotty." It's pretty hard to do. Even people who have never seen a single episode of *Star Trek* are totally familiar with this famous line.

Of course, the phrase has to do with *Star Trek*'s transporter beam. You see, in the world of *Star Trek* you don't have to take buses or cabs. If you want to go somewhere, you just step on a pad and the beam is activated. It breaks you down into energy, transmits that energy to a new location, and puts you back together there. Presto! You can go anywhere in a matter of seconds. It is just fiction, but remember we live in a world where we believe that anything that doesn't exist simply hasn't been invented yet.

HEY, WHERE'D EVERYBODY GO?

The transporter beam gives the world a context for people disappearing right before their very eyes. It means that when the rapture takes place, the first thing that will come to people's minds is *Star Trek*'s transporter beam. They will think that these people have been "beamed" away by someone. It will be the only frame of reference that they have. What an opportunity for the great deceiver to step forward, take credit for the vanishing, and then tell the survivors that he is here to lead them into a bold new world, "where no man has gone before."

Just think of all the possibilities that this *Star Trek* context will make available to the Antichrist whose goal is to deceive the whole world, and who has to begin by explaining something as incredible and unprecedented as the rapture.

The first thing he could tell the ones remaining is that the Christians had been holding the rest of the planet back. He could tell them that they are ready for the next step of enlightenment, maybe even the next step of human evolution, and now, with the Christians out of the way, there is nothing to stop them from discovering their destiny. Ours is a generation that would eat that up!

He might even tell the world that the Christians aren't gone forever. They're just in some kind of holding tank, being prepared for the realities of the new world. That would certainly soften the loss for those who had been left behind. What better way to ensure the loyalty of people who might otherwise be wallowing in anger and sorrow? Think about it. Imagine that your whole family suddenly vanishes, leaving you alone here on earth. Wouldn't you be a lot happier to hear that family members have been "beamed away" to get all this Christian nonsense out of their heads rather than think they're gone forever?

But the most important part of the Antichrist's whole deception surrounding the rapture is that there are no other logical explanations. We don't have any context within which to make sense of such an event, other than that provided by *Star Trek*'s transporter beam. The world might therefore follow the famous maxim of Sherlock Holmes and believe that "when you have excluded the impossible, whatever remains, however improbable, must be the truth." The *Star Trek* explanation might be all that remains.

Now, as we've said, *Star Trek* is certainly not alone in preparing the world for what lies ahead, nor are its producers making a conscious effort to prepare the world for an upcoming delusion. We merely want to point out that *Star Trek* has provided this world with a context for understanding the rapture. And as we saw in the last chapter, our context can have a tremendous impact on our interpretation of the events around us.

Could it really happen? Could people believe that such things are really possible? After all, we are talking about science fiction here. We can already hear the complaints of many science fiction fans: "It's just entertainment. What are you, nuts? Can't you tell the difference between television and the real world?"

THE PHYSICS OF *STAR TREK*: BLURRING THE LINE BETWEEN FANTASY AND REALITY

But wait a minute. In the world of *Star Trek* great care is taken to make it all sound so very logical and believable.

In creating the *Star Trek: The Next Generation* television series, the producers hired university professors in physics and other sciences to help them make everything sound possible. This mixture of fact and carefully designed fiction blurs the lines between what is real and what is possible. Thus, it should come as no surprise that in the minds of virtually all *Star Trek* fans, everything they see is quite possible; it's only a matter of time.

In the same way that people who have seen *Jurassic Park* think that the only thing standing in the way of creating real, live dinosaurs is a lack of dinosaur DNA, many also seem to think that the only thing standing in the way of traveling faster than the speed of light is the development of the dilithium crystals that power the *Enterprise.*

It all sounds so logical. And when the facts are presented in such a credible way, the fact that the presenter is a scientist from the twenty-third century, and that his words were penned by a fiction writer, can often be forgotten. Moreover, we can even find ourselves trying to remember whether we saw some incredible new piece of technology on *Star Trek* or on CNN!

POSSIBLE VS. PLAUSIBLE

You see, taken together, a myriad of factors—the fast pace of science, the expansion of knowledge, the increasing reliance on specialists in virtually every field, and the continuous bombardment of ideas from science fiction—has led us into a world where we can't tell the difference between what is *possible* and what is *plausible*.

And how can we possibly know where the lines between fantasy and reality lie today? What expertise do we have to make that determination? Think about your average evening at home. You pop a frozen dinner into the microwave and make your way into the living room, taking up your usual position in front of the television. You pick up the clicker and turn it on, flipping around the channels for a few minutes before deciding that there's nothing on. You reach for the other clicker on the coffee table and on comes the VCR. You press "play" and just like that you're watching a television program that was on last week in the middle of the night. If you really think about it, this is some pretty impressive technology that you're holding in the palm of your hand. But for most of us, we don't have a clue how it works, and we don't care. It's just something we take for granted.

Sometimes our total lack of awe that some of today's technology even exists is more amazing than the technology itself. The only time we give any real thought to the miracle of television, for example, is when we're thinking about getting a bigger one or a better one.

The reality of the situation is highlighted by the finding that roughly 95 percent of the American public can be considered scientifically illiterate by any rational standard. In this light it's no wonder that people get confused about what is fact and what is fiction. Add to that the fact that the quickly evolving technological world in which we live already makes it impossible to know everything about everything and we have the recipe for mass confusion and outright deception.

A DREAM AFRAID OF WAKING

A common reason that many young people give for enjoying *Star Trek* is that they "like the escape." But from what are they escaping? Most will tell you that it is from their perceived boredom with everyday life. Wow! As we've said, that's pretty amazing. Here we are, living smack in the middle of the most exciting and awe-inspiring time in history, and many of the youth of our day report being bored. Imagine putting today's kids on a seventeenth-century farm! It also raises the question of what exactly it is going to take to satisfy our seemingly insatiable hunger for something more.

So, maybe people are not just embracing the world of pseudoreality because they are confused. Maybe they are embracing it because they dearly want it to be true. An excellent book entitled *The Unreality Industry: The Deliberate Manufacturing of Falsehood and What It Is Doing to Our Lives* looked at this very issue, and authors Ian Mitroff and Warren Bennis concluded that this may very well be the case:

> We are inundated with shows that so blur the lines between reality and unreality that increasingly fewer of us either can *or care to* differentiate between them. Indeed, why care when *illusion is preferable* to a world/reality that has gotten even more difficult to manage. (Emphasis added)

How preferable has illusion become to reality? Well, how much time does the average American spend in front of the TV? Seven hours a day. That doesn't even count the time playing computer games or video games or watching movies. Ah, yes, we do love our illusion today. And as we'll see in another chapter down the road, a new form of illusion unlike anything the world has ever known is poised to bring us the ultimate illusion—virtual reality.

But boredom is not the only reason that so many souls are seeking answers in an illusionary reality. There is also a growing desire to get away from what might best be described as the harsh realities of everyday life. Too much war, too much crime, too much politics, too much violence, and as anyone who reads the daily paper can appreciate, the list could go on and on.

THE CHOICE OF A NEW GENERATION

Thus, another contributing factor in this choice of an entire generation to accept a new, though unreal, view of things comes from the fact that our world has become so complex that we can't figure it out. And when things get complex, we naturally try to put them in order. As Mitroff and Bennis point out in *The Unreality Industry*,

> It has also become clear that when the world can no longer be made coherent, either through explanation or action, then we seek coherence elsewhere. . . . As the outside world became increasingly complex . . . so that no one person or institution could fully understand or control it, we not only lost interest in dealing with reality per se but we invented substitute realities. . . . The fundamental purpose of all forms of unreality is to provide an illusion of control. If men cannot control the realities with which they are faced, then they will invent unrealities over which they can maintain an illusion of control.

Now, as we mentioned earlier, human beings do not like the idea of the gospel because we cannot control our own destiny. But in the world of *Star Trek*, we are the masters of our own fate; we can decide what is right and wrong, what is true and false. There is truly nothing else that can give us such an illusion of control.

HOW CAN REALITY COMPETE WITH FICTION?

So great is this anticipation for the great new world of *Star Trek* that it has made our real achievements (you know, the ones here in the real world) pale in comparison. We've already pointed out that a recent *Star Trek* exhibit at the Smithsonian Institution was one of its most popular shows ever. It drew much bigger crowds than the next room that merely contained real spacecraft (you know, the ones that went to the real moon).

Maybe this shouldn't surprise us. After all, how excited can you get about the space shuttle when you've just seen the starship *Enterprise* shooting through space at ten times the speed of light? As we'll discuss later, even the announcement that there may have been life on ancient Mars failed to get the kind of attention NASA was hoping for. Again, our expectations are so high that reality sometimes has a hard time keeping up. In the same way that *Baywatch* has made us a generation of people afraid to wear a bathing suit in public, *Star Trek* has made us very hard to impress with scientific breakthroughs.

Another point that's probably worth mentioning is the obvious difference in production value between the stuff we see on *Star Trek* and the stuff we get from NASA. Think about the footage of Neil Armstrong's historic first step on the moon. The greatest event in the history of television was grainy, black and white, and looked more like a home video than the ultimate culmination of a multibillion-dollar project to put men on the moon. But we are a generation in love with high production value, and anything less than full technicolor and stereo surround sound is totally unacceptable. This standard gives Hollywood another advantage over NASA when it comes to capturing our attention, and even though it's an advantage that we might not think about consciously, it plays a major role nonetheless.

Science fiction has had such an impact on our thinking, that even remarkable scientific discoveries in the real world often benefit from a little sensationalizing. As Stephen Hawking has said, "Black holes are an example, greatly assisted by the inspired name that the physicist John Archibald Wheeler gave them. Had they continued with their original names of 'frozen stars' or 'gravitationally completely collapsed objects,' there wouldn't have been half so much written about them."

HONEY, DON'T FORGET TO SPRAY-PAINT THE LAWN

It's not hard to see something of a self-sustaining cause-and-effect relationship here. Here we are, a little bit bored with reality, finding some measure of escape in the bold, new world of science fiction. While we're there, we are treated to wonderful breakthroughs and a refreshing look into the future, pushing the very limits of our imaginations. When we come back out, into the real world, do you think life looks more or less exciting than when we first turned on the TV? So, here we find ourselves, even more bored, and even more desirous for the wonderful world that science fiction has to offer. It's almost like an addictive drug; the more we get, the more we need to give us the same effect.

To see this effect more clearly, just take a look at the newest generation of action adventure movies. It's getting pretty hard for an action hero to really appear heroic. Don't forget, the new heroes don't just have to compete with those of us in the real world. That would be easy. Instead, they have to compete with one another. The Terminator has to outdo Indiana Jones, and Indiana Jones has to outdo Superman. And it's not just getting harder to find stuntmen and special effects that can keep up with the on-screen antics of our newest superheroes, but it's getting harder to think up the new stunts too.

In one recent movie, we see the heroes falling out of an airplane toward the frozen surface of a lake below. Faced with impending disaster, what do they do? They take out their pistols and shoot holes in the ice, falling safely into the water. Well, as you may recall, we are two young men who were raised in a place called North Bay, Ontario, Canada. We've seen ice, my friend, plenty of it, and you couldn't blow a hole in it with a cannon, let alone a pistol. But then again, isn't that the point of this entire chapter?

In a world where they spray-paint the grass with green paint on many football fields so that it looks more like real grass on TV, the world of illusion looks even more real than the one right in front of our eyes, but it is nonetheless a deceptive and imaginary world, created especially for this very generation.

CHAPTER 5

If a million people believe a foolish thing, it is still a foolish thing.

—Anatole France

WELCOME TO PLANET EARTH

I magine this. Tomorrow morning, a mysterious spaceship lands right in the middle of Times Square in New York City. The door opens, and a mysterious-looking creature climbs out and, in the true spirit of the *Star Trek* generation, starts talking in perfect English. The whole world would be watching, just as we do all great events, like the assassination of John F. Kennedy, Neil Armstrong's first small step for man, or the slow-speed chase of O. J. Simpson's Ford Bronco. The alien then informs us that he is not only from another planet, but from another *time* as well! You see, this little green man has come to us from the future and wants to warn us about a major catastrophe that is about to befall us. And now for the $64,000 question: Do we believe him?

Before you think about that any further, let us ask you one more question: Do you think more people would believe him tomorrow than would have believed him if he had arrived a hundred years ago? At first blush, most people think he would have had better success a hundred years ago, when we were less sophisticated. "It would have been easy to fool those scientifically ignorant people," you say.

In reality, all of our incredible knowledge and sophistication has only made us *more* likely to believe him today than we would have at any time in the past. Why? Because his story now *seems plausible*, even though it might not seem (or be) *possible*. To return to what we talked about earlier, we also have a context within which to organize our thoughts about this event. A hundred years ago, there was no such context. There was no space shuttle, *Apollo 11*, *Star Trek*, *E.T.*, or *Star Wars*. The list could go on and on. Trying to make sense of something totally new is always a lot more difficult when you don't have any framework to fit it in. Remember, without the proper context, people in London, England, couldn't even cope with an escalator.

TONIGHT, ON A VERY SPECIAL *LARRY KING* . . .

Okay, so now we have the world divided, half believing him and half not. That night, the alien appears on the *Larry King Live* show, along with several prominent intellectuals from NASA and various institutes of higher learning. One of them tells us that Einstein's theory of relativity does not preclude the possibility of time travel. A graphic on screen shows how time is made up of waves, allowing thousands of years to be skipped by traveling from crest to crest rather than following the wave up and down. Three other guys agree with the math, and all agree that it is certainly possible. Suddenly, you'd have the whole world on one side. Well, almost the whole world. There would still be groups, characterized as idiots by the press, who would argue that it was some kind of conspiracy. But for the most part, we'd go to work examining what he had to say and figuring out how to avoid the future catastrophe that he so kindly warned us about.

The point is this. No matter what people claim right now, we'd be all over this alien, not only because his story seemed plausible, but also because we've been expecting him. And because we've so badly been wanting him to come.

Given that Satan is referred to in the Bible as "the prince of the power of the air" (Eph. 2:2) and that he comes to deceive the world with "all power and signs and lying wonders," (2 Thess. 2:9) the potential for deception is staggering.

> *One of the surest signs that intelligent life exists in outer space is that none of it has tried to contact us.*
>
> *—Normandy Alden*

Jacques Vallee, considered by many to be the top UFO expert in the world, has concluded that while UFO's do appear to be real, they do not appear to be physical. Could it be that the entire UFO phenomenon is a carefully orchestrated deception used by Satan to deceive the last days world? Once again, Jacques Vallee noted the possibility:

> Some witnesses have thought they had seen demons because the creatures had the unpredictability and mischievousness associated with popular conceptions of the devil. If you wanted to bypass the intelligencia and church, remain undetectable to the military system, leave undisturbed the political and administrative levels of society, and at the same time implant deep within that society far reaching doubts concerning its basic philosophical tenets, this is exactly how you would have to act. . . . This is exactly what the UFO phenomenon does.

LOOKING FOR HOPE IN ALL THE WRONG PLACES

There is no doubt that something's going on! TV shows such as the *X-Files*, *Star Trek*, and *Third Rock from the Sun* are rapidly becoming the most popular (and profitable) programs on television. Movies such as *Independence Day* and *Phenomenon* are drawing record crowds into the theaters. Less than two months after its release in July 1996, *Independence Day* (with the interesting subtitle "The End Is Here") had already grossed almost a quarter of a billion dollars. Obviously, the world is hungry for hope and ready to take the next giant step into the future. Unfortunately, however, as we will see, while many of the world's people *do* have their eyes on the skies, they're looking for the wrong savior.

Sure, there have always been seekers, visiting psychics, watching the skies for UFO's, and seeking guidance from the spirit world. But today, things have moved into the mainstream, and it is becoming an increasingly important part of our generation. Even the White House isn't immune to this incredible shift in what is being deemed acceptable. No sooner had Nancy Reagan and her team of astrologers moved out of the White House than Hillary Clinton and her personal psychic Jean Houston moved in. According to well-publicized reports, Houston helped Mrs. Clinton conduct séances with the spirits of several dead people, including Eleanor Roosevelt and Mahatma Gandhi. When pressed, the first lady denied that they were actual séances, and Houston insisted that Mrs. Clinton is actually a very "committed Christian" and a "serious, reflective, and prayerful woman." So what's she doing sitting in the Oval Office having tea with dead people? Simple. She's caught up in the same wave of spiritualism that's sweeping the entire nation.

Does this mean that Mrs. Clinton is lying about being a Christian? No, not necessarily. One of the most alarming trends that we're seeing today is the increasing tendency of Christians to combine their faith with an assortment of New Age beliefs. A recent Gallup poll examined this trend and found that nearly 50 percent of all American Christians believed in psychic healing, and more than 25 percent believed in astrology! So, Mrs. Clinton is not really "out there," as many people have implied. Instead, there she is, right where she wants to be, in the cultural mainstream.

IMAGINATION ON OVERDRIVE

Once again, we can't overlook how these Hollywood images are transforming our ideas about UFO's. Ten years ago anyone who talked about UFO's was snickered at. Today, the discussion of contact is very real. As Stephen Hawking, one of the world's most prominent scientists, has noted, "Science fiction like *Star Trek* is not only good fun but it also serves a serious purpose, that of expanding the human imagination."

This same thought was echoed by Edwin (Buzz) Aldrin, one of the *Apollo 11* astronauts and the second man to walk on the moon. Paying tribute to the *Star Trek* series on a prime-time special commemorating the show's thirtieth anniversary, Aldrin called the "expansion of the American imagination" *Star Trek*'s greatest contribution. A colleague added that *Star Trek*'s role was vital since "fantasy is the stepping-stone to reality." As we're going to see, this expansion of our beliefs about what is possible is going to play a key role in this incredible generation.

READY, WILLING, AND WAITING

The idea of aliens from outer space visiting us here on planet earth is not new. During the last few years of the last century, H. G. Wells had the whole world watching for Martians. Now, here we are, a hundred years later, still watching for visitors from another world, only this time, we're watching a lot more closely.

And is the world really ready for contact? According to

Tom Jennings, we certainly are. And who, you might ask, is Tom Jennings? He is the mayor of Roswell, New Mexico, a small town near the site of a supposed UFO crash in 1947. Today, more than 75,000 tourists visit Roswell each year to see the crash site and visit the town's UFO Museum and Research Center, strategically situated right in the town square. According to the grateful mayor, it doesn't really matter if a UFO ever landed or not; the whole thing has been a boost for the local economy.

The television ratings also suggest that the world might be ready for a message from the skies. The television series the *X-Files* has become one of the most popular programs of our day, and it deals almost exclusively with the government investigation and cover-up of alien encounters. And as we have already discussed, futuristic

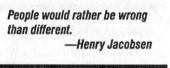

People would rather be wrong than different.
—Henry Jacobsen

programs such as *Star Trek* and *Babylon 5* continue to make the whole idea of intelligent life elsewhere in the universe a little easier to swallow back here on earth.

Nevada drivers may also be getting the message during a drive through the countryside, especially if they decide to take Nevada State Route 375, which was recently renamed the Extraterrestrial Highway. Located just outside the top secret air force base known as Area 51, this highway is about to be graced with a monument designed to serve as a homing beacon for visitors from other planets.

Even though much of this is just fun and games, an important message is in there somewhere. It is that the world is ready, willing, and waiting for a visit from E.T.

NOT JUST FUN AND GAMES

On a more serious front, giant satellite dishes have been erected, at considerable expense, to do nothing but listen to the sky. Every day, every night, around the clock, they listen and listen and listen. For what? For some kind of sign that intelligent life exists outside our own little world.

In the day of tight budgets and growing deficits you would think there would be opposition to the funding of such an esoteric project. But that's not the case. As we've noted, a recent *Time*/CNN poll discovered that one in three American adults actually expects that we'll be contacted by aliens in the next hundred years. Even when federal cutbacks in the early nineties promised to cut off entire arms of government, politicians were careful to note that NASA's budget would not be significantly reduced.

> *No matter what happens, the U.S. Navy is not going to be caught napping.*
> *—Secretary of the Navy Frank Knox, December 5, 1941*

So far, these giant microphones to the heavens haven't actually heard anything of much interest, but recently, the E.T. watchers did get a boost when NASA announced the possible discovery of evidence for life on ancient Mars. You would have thought that such an incredible "discovery" would have sent the world into a frenzy of excitement, but unfortunately for NASA fund-raisers, the reaction was less than enthusiastic. The big question, of course, is *why*.

LIFE ON MARS? WHO CARES?

One possible explanation is that the evidence was not exactly exciting. You see, they didn't actually find life on Mars. The life that they found was right here on earth in the frozen waste of Antarctica.

In a nutshell, here is the story as NASA scientists told it to the world. About 15 million years ago a giant asteroid smashed into the planet Mars, making quite a mess in the process. Not only did it send rocks and dirt flying in every direction on the planet's surface, but the intensity of the collision was so great, it actually sent stuff flying clear out into space. One such rock drifted aimlessly in space for almost the entire time since then, until, about 13,000 years ago, it fell to the earth and landed somewhere in the frozen tundra of the earth's south pole. Some years ago, scientists found the rock, dug it out of the ice, and brought it home as a souvenir. There it sat, undergoing careful study, but mostly just sitting there.

Then, years later, someone took another look at the rock with a new, more powerful microscope, and that's when they found it. What was it? A footprint? A fossilized skull of an alien creature? Not exactly. What they had was something that sort of looked like something that may have sort of resembled the shape of microscopic bacteria. No wonder the world was bored by this discovery. There were few signs of excitement. NASA was excited that it might get a nice boost in its budget. President Clinton was excited that it was an American discovery, and, he was quick to get in front of the television cameras to proclaim that the "implications are as far-reaching and awe-inspiring as can be imagined." Actually, the president's statement summed up the mood of the world. The discovery itself wasn't all that exciting, but the *implications* of that discovery, well, that's another story.

And it didn't take long for the media to bring all kinds of people out of the woodwork, giving us their little "spin" on the life on Mars story. Wes Huntress of the Johnson Space Center noted that the discovery "means that life originated on a planet other than our own . . . and if it originated on more than one planet in this solar system, why wouldn't it have originated in some other solar system?" Another scientist speculated that life here on earth may have been seeded by a meteorite like that one. In other words, maybe we're all Martians!

THE SEARCH FOR LITTLE GREEN MEN

Finally, before we move away from this topic, we should clarify that for every scientist marveling at the discovery of life on Mars, there is at least one marveling at the fact that other scientists are marveling at the discovery of life on Mars. These skeptics point out that NASA may have jumped the gun a little bit, announcing something as important as this with surprisingly little evidence.

Even in their initial meeting with the press, NASA officials admitted that the shapes they saw may have been bacteria from Antarctica here on earth or maybe even dried mud! Whatever those shapes may have been, it appeared to many that the little green men NASA was looking for may have been George Washington, Thomas Jefferson, and Benjamin Franklin. Actually, on the subject of money, no one was happier with NASA's announcement than the producers of the motion picture *Independence Day*. It would be hard to quantify the effect of this publicity on their ticket sales, but you'd be pretty safe to bet that it was substantial.

BETTING ON E.T.

As for timing, this latest "discovery" couldn't have come at a better time. Here we are, about to begin not only a new century, but also a new millennium, and the world is really, really ready for something like this. Consider the story of a gentleman in Britain, who won $1,540 with a bet he placed in August of 1995 that alien life would be discovered within a year. He could have won a lot more money in a world not so anxious for contact.

You see, the bookmaker William Hill said he had cut the odds on discovery of extraterrestrial life from 500–1 to 25–1 and finally 10–1, where it was at the time of the bet.

Think about that. Hill didn't cut the odds based on an intensified search or some new discovery. The only thing that had changed was us and our own expectations. A bumper sticker commonly sold at UFO conventions sums up the situation very well. It says simply, "I want to believe."

To see just how far we've really come in our belief that there may be something to this whole UFO thing after all, consider that the Federal Emergency Management Agency (FEMA) is using a training manual that includes a section on dealing with UFO situations. The manual, *The Fire Officer's Guide to Disaster Control*, is used by many local fire departments in disaster planning. Chapter 13 of that manual, with the title "Enemy Attack and UFO Potential," begins with the words "In this chapter we will now turn our attention to the very real threat posed by Unidentified Flying Objects (UFO's) whether they exist or not."

So why is the world so anxious to find (and certain that we will) signs of life outside our own planet? Well, for one thing, we're bored. Simple as that. Don't forget, this is the generation that is seeing the sum of our knowledge double every two years. When things move that quickly, as we've discussed earlier, one result is a staggering reduction in our attention spans. We're a generation constantly starved for something new, something bigger, something faster all the time. We've become conditioned to expect, and even need, change. And lots of it.

A cartoon hanging in our offices illustrates the situation very well. It shows a little boy standing in front of a microwave. He is holding a package in his hand, and he is shouting toward his mother, "Two minutes!!?? I thought you said it was instant!" Such is the state of the world today. Nothing is good enough. Nothing is fast enough. And certainly, it's going to take a lot more than a fossil that may have at some time looked similar to something

that may at some time have something to do with life. We
want aliens. We want flying saucers. We want intelligent,
English-speaking, highly advanced creatures to come to
earth and lead us into the next millennium.

YOU SAW A FLYING SAUCER? BIG DEAL!
I'VE BEEN *IN* ONE!

It's interesting, too, that in this generation, UFO
sightings are no longer the order of the day. Instead, we
are hearing more and more about alien *abductions*. It's as
if seeing a flying saucer isn't good enough anymore.
Remember, this is the "been there, done that" generation.
Always wanting something bigger and better than the day
before. Statistics gathered by the United States Air Force
show that almost four million Americans claim to have
been abducted by aliens. Think about that. Four million
Americans! Wow!

But for many, even that isn't good enough. One
"abductee," frustrated that even the tabloid TV talk shows
weren't all that interested in his story, complained that
even being abducted by a UFO isn't sensational enough
anymore, "Now you have to have alien babies."
Fortunately for this frustrated fellow, there is some solace.
He can share his woes with others in one of the dozens of
alien abduction support groups that have sprung up
around the country. Check your yellow pages. Maybe
there is one in your area.

THE POWER OF THE NEW MILLENNIUM

With the approach of the year 2000, this incredible
hunger for something very big to happen is going to
become even more pronounced. And for an increasing
number of people in this generation, a good old-fashioned
close encounter with aliens may be just what the doctor

ordered. Why? Because it gives us answers to some of the biggest questions of all time. Are we alone? Why are we here? And the big one, where did we come from?

As the quest for answers continues, and as the world searches harder and harder for signs of life elsewhere in the universe, keeping one important fact in mind is critical. *Believing* that there is life "out there" can have the same effect as there actually *being* life "out there." Please take a second to read that last sentence again. It is essential to understanding the *real* power of the UFO phenomenon. That power lies in the fact that in today's world it is not so important whether UFO's exist as whether we believe they exist. And one in three Americans actually *expects* that we'll be contacted by aliens within the next century.

THE POWER TO DECEIVE THE WHOLE WORLD

In the light of Bible prophecy, the significance of this possibility becomes clear. Remember, we would be dealing with a supernatural event. We are talking about Satan himself, with the power to deceive the whole world. And the world doesn't have to be deceived by cheap tricks like smoke and mirrors. Not by a long shot.

The Bible tells us that even the strongest believers who have ever lived would be deceived by the carefully crafted last days deception—if they were here and if God allowed it. Think about what the Bible is telling us. We're talking about Moses, Noah, or the apostle Paul. A deception that powerful should not be underestimated.

Added to this great power to deceive is another very significant factor: The victims of this deception actually *want* to be deceived. They are down here, living in this time of unparalleled knowledge and discovery, and just starving for something big like this to happen. They want, more than anything else, answers to their biggest questions, and they want desperately for that answer to be *anything but God*!

An encounter with extraterrestrial life, or at least a seeming encounter with extraterrestrial life, would be the basis for the greatest challenge to Christianity in the history of this planet. Overnight it would change the way people view themselves, the earth, their origins, the universe, and the future!

We'll talk more about this possible scenario a little later in the book. For the time being, just recognize how the world is indeed being set up for a deception beyond even our wildest imaginations. Not only could it easily explain the rapture, but it could provide the world with a powerful and more acceptable gospel in one fell swoop.

CHAPTER 6

*The obvious question is what to do with VR. The short
answer is anything you want.*

—Insight, *May 6, 1991*

VIRTUAL REALITY

Deception comes in many forms, and before we start thinking that we need a UFO to land in order to deceive this world, let's take a look at something much closer to home. It may even be sitting on your desk right now.

Virtual reality has long been considered the "Holy Grail" of the computer and technology world. And even today, with breakthroughs coming at an almost unimaginable pace in every area of science, few hold the promise and excitement of VR. When you think about it, though, this shouldn't come as a very big surprise. We are, after all, a generation who covets experience above all else, and when a new technology comes along that promises *experience without consequences*, then people are certainly going to sit up and take notice.

Before we go a whole lot farther, let's take a few minutes to find out what VR is really all about. We'd like to start by giving you a sneak preview of a scene from a screenplay that we've been working on that will one day bring the message of Bible prophecy to the big screen.

In this scene, CIA agent Thorold Stone arrives for a meeting at the home of his new partner, Willy Holmes.

EXTERIOR—JUST BEFORE DUSK—WILLY'S HOUSE
This is a white-picket-fence house. Totally ordinary but well out in the country. It almost looks like an older woman could live there. Only the Harley in the driveway indicates otherwise. Thorold pulls his K car in beside the bike and walks up onto the front porch. There is a straw welcome mat at the door. As he opens the screen door Thorold hears a series of gunshots ring out in the house. He assumes defensive posture beside the door and draws his gun. He then slowly pushes the door fully open.

INTERIOR—WILLY'S HOUSE—ENTRANCEWAY
Thorold cautiously enters the house. More shots ring out.

INTERIOR—WILLY'S HOUSE—LIVING ROOM
He rolls from the hallway into the living room, but nothing is there. More shots are fired in the back room. He makes his way to the back room doorway and puts his back to the wall just outside it. He then hears Willy speaking:

Willy

Oh, I know what you're thinking. Did he fire six shots, or did he fire only five? You got to ask yourself, do you feel lucky?

Thorold recognizes the famous Clint Eastwood line and kind of cocks his head, wondering.

INTERIOR—WILLY'S HOUSE—BACK ROOM
He crouches low and swings around the door behind his leveled gun to reveal Willy decked out in an all-white cowboy suit complete with all the trimmings, a pair of six-shooters, and wearing homemade-looking virtual reality goggles. He is standing on a round VR roller mill. Thorold smiles, but his smile quickly vanishes as Willy swings around his way, gun leading. Thorold yells. This scares Willy who also screams. He rips off his goggles, and they face each other.

Willy
Thorold!

Thorold
(imitating John Wayne)
Who were ya expecting, Pilgrim?

Computer Voice
You have just been fatally shot.

Willy
Rats!

Computer Voice
Do you wish to try again?

Willy
Not tonight, Mia.

Thorold is regaining his composure and marveling at the equipment in the room.

Thorold
This is really something!

Willy
Here, try this.

He hands him a duplicate set of goggles and motions for him to set up on the unit beside him. Thorold puts on the goggles . . .

EXTERIOR—DAY—VIRTUAL REALITY BEACH
and instantly sees Willy, wearing swim trunks, standing in front of him on a beach. The ambience is perfect. He looks down at himself. He can't believe it. He touches his stomach. Then he bends and touches the water. More amazement. He picks up some sand and slowly pours it out

of his hand. He picks up some more, rises, and reaches up to his eyes as if he's lifting the goggles.

INTERIOR—WILLY'S HOUSE—BACK ROOM; THOROLD'S POINT OF VIEW
He looks and sees his hand with no sand. He also looks over and sees Willy rubbing his arm. He replaces the goggles and is . . .

EXTERIOR—DAY—VIRTUAL REALITY BEACH
back at the beach and Willy is spreading lotion on his arm.

> **Willy**
> (very casually)

Lotion?

> **Thorold**

Do I need it?

> **Willy**

No more than I needed the cowboy suit.

> **Thorold**
> (looking around)

Man, if I had one of these, I'd never leave the house.

> **Willy**

Why do you think I work at home?

They begin to walk in the surf down the beach.

> **Willy**

Let's stroll. I've narrowed down where our mysterious viruses are coming from. I haven't been able to pinpoint it exactly but it is coming from a twelve-square-mile area near L.A.

> **Thorold**

How much narrower can you get it?

Willy calls out to his computer.

> **Willy**
> Mia, bring me the virus files.

A pretty girl up on the beach brings him a manila folder. She has a red beehive hairdo. He takes it and refers to it.

> **Willy**
> Give me a couple of days, and I can tell you what room he's in. Mia's working on it now.

> **Thorold**
> Great.

They walk quietly for a bit. Thorold is still looking all around, freaked out at what he's seeing.

> **Thorold**
> (looking at watch)
> Maybe we should start heading back.

> **Willy**
> (laughing)
> That's the beauty of this thing. We don't have to head back. We just have to leave.

He reaches up and takes off his goggles. Thorold sees Willy vanish from the beach in front of him. He too lifts his visor from his face and . . .

INTERIOR—WILLY'S HOUSE—BACK ROOM
we see the two men standing in Willy's back room again.

> **Thorold**
> What a great toy that is! I feel like I just took a nice walk on the beach.

Willy

Yeah, and it helps me to remember that appearances can be deceiving.

SO, WHAT IS VIRTUAL REALITY?

The story of Willy and Thorold gives us a look at the worlds that virtual reality technology will open up. Virtual reality refers to the computer technology that allows you to move through and interact with a three-dimensional, computer-generated environment. Generally, here's how it works. You put on a pair of special computer-equipped goggles that look sort of like an oversized set of welding glasses. Little TV screens, one in front of each eye, give you a view of a computer-created image. Each eye receives a slightly different image, and this gives you the illusion of three dimensions (in other words, depth perception).

Stop reading right now. Cover your left eye with your hand, and look at this page with only your right eye. Now, cover your right eye, and look at the page only with your left eye. Notice that the actual view in each eye is slightly different. (You may want to switch back and forth quickly a few times to really appreciate this fact.) By mimicking the workings of the world's greatest computer, the human brain, virtual reality systems attempt, quite successfully, to create the perception of depth.

But that's not the end of it. These VR helmets also have sensitive mechanisms built into them that can detect even slight movements of your head. When you turn your head to look to the left, the computer updates the screens in front of your eyes so that the virtual world appears to move as you do. Let's say you're going to take a virtual walk on the surface of the moon. You walk into a VR lab and take your place on a treadmill. You put on your helmet/goggles, and you're ready to go. The computer starts up, and right in front of your eyes, on those two little screens, is a perfect representation of the moon. You look up, and you see the black sky, a million stars, and even the beautiful blue earth, hanging in space. You look down, and you see the dusty surface of the moon surrounding an image of your virtual feet. You look left, and you see some craters and a small hill. You look right, and you see the abandoned dune buggy, gold foil glimmering, left behind by *Apollo 14* astronauts. You can even (thanks to the treadmill) walk all the way around that moon buggy. As far as your eyes are concerned, you are really there.

This is a very simplistic description of virtual reality, but it should give you an idea of just what we're talking about. Once you start adding bells and whistles, the experience can become incredibly real. How real? Well, let's just say that airline pilots are now trained in virtual reality simulators that are so real they are allowed to take their first flight in a real airplane with passengers on board. You see, in the very best VR systems, your eyes are only the beginning of the illusion.

A FULL-COURSE BUFFET FOR YOUR SENSES

A company in Arizona offers a device called the Experience System that is a virtual reality game system with lots of realism built in. It has a very high-resolution display for your eyes, stereophonic headphones for your ears, a heat-sensitive chair for your body, a glove for your hand that can actually manipulate objects in the virtual world, and even a hose that fits under your nose emitting smells as you wander around in cyberspace! Imagine the realism you could experience under these conditions.

You start up the machine, and you see in front of you a dark street with a few people walking around. Suddenly, you hear a loud explosion behind you and feel a flash of heat on your back. You turn around and see a car that has burst into flames about twenty feet away. You can hear someone calling for help from inside, and you run over and reach for the door. You see your hand grab the handle and you feel the heat in your fingers. You pull open the door and have to step back as a flash of heat rushes over your entire body. The smell of smoke is overwhelming, but you fight through it anyway and reach inside the car and grab the clothing of the passenger in the front seat. He is heavier than you thought he might be, and you feel his weight as you pull him from the car. As you drag him along the pavement, you are actually straining under the load, and you get him out of range just in time. The car explodes into a ball of flame, sending you flying onto your virtual derriere. You feel the pain as you meet the pavement, and then reach up and lift off the goggles. There you are, sitting in a VR lab, covered in sweat, but none the worse for wear. That is virtual reality.

And this is not science fiction. Some fire departments and emergency response teams have already installed sophisticated virtual reality systems to train their personnel for real-life emergencies. And as we'll see, this is only the beginning of what virtual reality can be used for.

LET'S TALK TURKEY

Imagine sitting around the dinner table at Thanksgiving. Your family enjoys the company of everyone, separated throughout the year by geography. But tonight, you're all together again, or so it seems. In actuality, you're sitting alone in your living room, wearing your trusty VR suit and goggles. Your brother, seated to your left and asking you to pass the virtual potatoes, is in Washington. Your sister and her husband are in Florida. Your parents are in Virginia, and your grandparents are in London, England. And yet, here you sit, all "together" in a virtual world.

According to most experts, such a scenario is not far off. The technology to make it a reality is already here, but like many new technologies, it remains too expensive for the average person to have in the home. Like everything in the world of technology, however, this high cost is changing fast, and thanks to enormous investments on the part of the electronic games industry, VR could be a household reality within a very short time. Virtual "travel" like this may become the norm within a few years and could truly bring the world to your living room without your having to even leave the house.

DON'T LOOK DOWN!

Sound great? Well, it is. And in the VR world, this is only the beginning. Psychologists are using VR to treat a number of phobias, including the ever-so-common acrophobia, the fear of heights. Patients can go through a series of VR therapy sessions that take them to the tops of ladders and buildings and even into virtual airplanes. And just how real are these virtual experiences? Patients report the initial experiences to be so real that most experience sweaty palms, rubbery knees, and even vomiting! The good news, though, is that after about three weeks of virtual sessions, more than 90 percent of patients have reported a significant reduction in their fears.

Imagine being able to confront and work through your fears in a virtual world. You see, the experience itself is every bit as frightening as it would have been in the real world, but there are no consequences. If you fall off the Sears Tower, it's no big deal. You just pick yourself up and climb right back on.

And acrophobia is only one of the fears being treated in this way. You can handle virtual spiders, pet virtual dogs, make virtual public speeches before a crowd of thousands, and even swim with virtual sharks.

Practice Makes Perfect

VR also has tremendous value to people needing to practice skills before taking them into the real world. We've already talked about airline pilots learning to fly virtual jets before ever taking control of a real one. Surgeons are also using VR to practice delicate surgical procedures before attempting them on a real person. Imagine the advantage to a brain surgeon of having removed a tumor from a virtual brain fifteen times before ever attempting it on a real, live brain.

Architects are using VR to allow them to "walk through" the buildings they design, making sure that everything looks just right, and that every door is just where it should be. They can even make sure that the whole building is accessible to people with disabilities, and all before a single brick is laid.

By using remote-controlled robots in combination with virtual reality technology, scientists have developed systems that allow people to carry out very dangerous tasks from a distance. Whether it be cleaning up after a nuclear meltdown, rescuing someone from a burning building, disposing of a bomb, or exploring the deepest depths of the sea, VR allows you to be "right there," at least virtually. As novelist William Gibson said of VR, "There is no there, there."

Clearly, VR is an unbelievable technology, and we should be doing everything we can to make it better and more affordable, right? Well, as in so many areas of life, the answer is a resounding yes and no. And like every technology to have come along in the last one hundred years, there is always a dark side. Let's turn our attention to that aspect of VR right now.

Virtual Violence

One of the big issues in the world of VR is violence. What are the ethics involved in virtual rape and murder?

And if you have any doubt about whether or not VR will ever move in that direction, then all you have to do is take a quick look at the computer game industry.

In the PC world, games such as DOOM, Mortal Kombat, and Quake are little more than 3-D worlds (on the computer screen) in which the player runs through hallways, opening doors and shooting everything that moves. To make the adventure more realistic, the victims squirt blood when shot and even cry out in pain. In one game, Rise of the Triad, Nazi soldiers are the enemy, and to win the game, you have to kill them all. Often, during the course of the game, you may wound a soldier but not actually kill him. The wounded man falls to his knees and waves his hands in the air saying, "No, please, don't shoot, please, please don't shoot." If you don't shoot him, however, he will pull out a gun and *shoot you*. In other words, if you don't kill this guy, with his hands in the air, begging for his life, then you will lose the game!

> *As computing power continues to get cheaper, the technology will enter everyday lives. Within a decade people will be taking utterly realistic vacations to other countries—or even other worlds. They'll learn to operate sophisticated machinery without ever touching it. And their kids will be playing video games that make Sonic the Hedgehog and Super Mario Brothers seem as exciting as silent movies.*
> —Time, *July 17, 1995*

TWENTY MILLION "DOOMED"

In the wildly popular game DOOM, you travel through corridors and castles hunting down your enemies and killing them with everything from knives and shotguns to rocket launchers and even a chain saw. Conservative estimates put the number of players of this game at somewhere in the area of twenty million people worldwide. And if players get tired of shooting or otherwise maiming the computer-supplied enemies, then the game is equipped for modem or network play. What does this mean? It means that now you can shoot and maim your friends too. Let's face it. In the world of modern computer gaming, violence is in, and the more blood, the better.

On the surface, there are the obvious issues of overexposure to gratuitous violence. That debate has raged since the earliest days of television and is likely to continue for some time to come. The arguments by supporters of TV and computer violence have always been pretty much the same. First, there is the old "if you don't like it, turn it off" approach, which seems reasonable enough for responsible adults. But when it comes to kids who may not know what's best for them, the argument must be amended to something like "this is clearly just entertainment, any competent person can tell the difference between this and reality." Well, in the world of virtual reality, this second argument may begin to break down.

HUMAN TARGET PRACTICE

An interesting study done near the end of the Second World War may shed some light on this rather important issue. A group of U.S. Army researchers conducted private, confidential interviews with veterans of combat during that war. Those studies revealed the shocking fact that only 15 to 20 percent of those soldiers who faced actual combat ever fired their weapons in battle. Less than 5 percent of the soldiers did the vast majority of the killing. Well, to say the least, this finding stunned and shocked military leaders, who looked into the matter a little further. Poring over historical documents, they found that even during the Battle of Gettysburg, in 1863, 90 percent of the abandoned muskets picked up after the battle had been loaded but not fired.

Obviously, these revelations were very troubling to military officials, and they decided to take steps to get to the root of the problem. One of the approaches that they tried (with tremendous success) was to replace the paper bull's-eye targets used during shooting practice with more realistic-looking human pop-up targets. The results were staggering. During the Vietnam War, 95 percent of soldiers were firing their weapons in battle, which could explain the increase in the number of soldiers returning home with severe psychological problems. Clearly, more realistic representations made it easier for soldiers to repeat what they had learned in practice in the real world.

A report on this phenomenon noted:

> The military have developed techniques to overcome this resistance [to kill], but it's not only the military who are using them. All the industrialized societies are now unintentionally subjecting their young to the same techniques, with the same results. We are teaching the kids to kill. (*Hamilton Spectator*, December 8, 1995)

You see, if soldiers were more willing to use their weapons against another human being after practicing on human-looking pop-up targets, then what happens to kids who kill literally thousands of even more realistic-looking people on a computer screen? And now, what about virtual reality?

A LITTLE SOMETHING EXTRA FOR THE TEACHER

Consider this scenario. Little Johnny comes home from school after being scolded by his teacher for not having done his homework. He goes into his bedroom and turns on his computer. He throws on the VR helmet and gloves and dives full speed into his own virtual world. In that world, he walks into his classroom and sees his teacher at the front of the class. Casually, he strolls down the aisle, lifts the double-barreled shotgun in front of him, and blows his teacher into a million bits, even as the teacher is begging for his life.

I think you'd have to agree that this is a quantum leap beyond violence on TV or even games such as DOOM. And even more frightening, the technology to make it all possible exists already. It's only a matter of time until VR becomes cheap enough to be as common as VCR's and personal computers are today.

WHEN THE THRILL IS GONE

With the ability to kill an unlimited number of people in virtual reality, all without any consequences whatsoever, it's not hard to imagine cases arising of people suddenly finding that the virtual thrill is no longer quite enough. How long will it take these people to move up the ladder and start doing their killing in the real world? Before you start thinking that we're really reaching here, consider once again the effect on soldiers of using human-looking targets. Even more amazing, consider that twice as many people were shot in the United States during the Vietnam War than were shot in Vietnam. We're living in a world already far too prone to violence. Many people are living a lot closer to the edge than we might like to think.

Chances are, the issues we're raising here might sound a little familiar. After all, isn't this the same stuff we heard about television, movies, and pornography? Well, in a way, the answer has to be yes. But in the VR world, we're talking about something much more dangerous. You see, in virtual reality, that distinction between what is real and what is not is blurred, and the whole experience is much more intense. Watching a guy get shot on TV is a lot different from shooting him yourself in a realistic virtual world. And think about how much more difficult that distinction will be for people with preexisting psychological or emotional problems.

I JUST CAN'T STOP

There are a lot of other issues for us to think about besides violence when considering the potential impact of the incredible new VR technologies. One of the most important, and you've probably thought about this one, is addiction. Just think about it. Imagine introducing this technology to a generation like ours. A generation that covets experience above all else. And a generation that will do almost anything to escape from boredom. Let's face it. We're not an easy generation to entertain. Suddenly, a new technology comes along that provides the ultimate answer to a thrill-seeking generation. The implications could be far-reaching.

McGill University psychologist Glenn Cartwright has studied the impact of VR technology in depth and states, "If you become an ideal person in the virtual world, then have to come back and be the same old person that you were, that could be very depressing." Depressing? Talk about an understatement. You go into this world, and suddenly, you are like a god there. You can do what you want, create any scenario you desire. You can be the smartest, fastest, strongest, and sexiest. You can be a foot taller or a hundred pounds lighter, and have the good looks of your favorite movie star. You can kill anyone who annoys you, have your enemies worship you, even make love to anyone you desire. Frankly, it's going to be a little tough to come out of that world to head into your job frying hamburgers at McDonald's.

LIKE MAINLINING TELEVISION

So, will VR become addictive? Well, let's look at television for a comparison. The average North American adult now spends an average of seven hours a day watching television. By the time that same person is thirty-five years old, he'll have spent almost nine full years in front of the television set! And television is a totally passive medium, where we watch what's on, not what we'd like to watch. If there is nothing on that interests us, we watch anyway. Virtual reality will be like mainlining television. Imagine how much more TV you'd watch if you could get right inside your favorite programs and interact with the characters. Suddenly, you're right there in Jerry Seinfeld's living room, laughing along with George, Elaine, and Kramer. Or maybe you'd prefer to be a member of the emergency room staff on *ER*. How about joining Indiana Jones for an exciting adventure in the Egyptian pyramids? It's hard to imagine the majority of us ever leaving the house.

A couple of years ago we held a prophecy conference in Anaheim, California, and like most of those attending from out of town, we found time to slip over to Universal Studios for an afternoon of relaxation. One of the rides there was called Back to the Future, and it was something quite close to a VR experience. In that ride, passengers sit in a car equipped with hydraulic lifts that allow it to rock back and forth, thrust forward, and tilt in every direction, giving a true illusion of movement.

When the ride starts, all the lights go out, and your entire field of view is filled with a high-definition movie screen in front of you. As your "flying car" soars through the movie, you actually feel as if you're flying. If you ever get a chance to experience this ride, please do; it's worth the wait. Despite forty-five-minute waiting lines, we both went back four or five times.

ADONIS IN WONDERLAND

But addiction is not the only issue likely to face us as VR becomes part of our everyday lives. Let's take a few minutes now to consider some of the moral implications. Once VR becomes interactive in nature, allowing more than one person to "exist" in the same virtual environment, then deception is pretty much guaranteed to become the rule rather than the exception. Just think about it. If you are able in this virtual world to present yourself in any way you want, are you likely to choose the real you? If you can honestly answer yes, then you're a lot more secure in your self-image than the rest of us. Actually meeting someone face-to-face will become pretty rare. First of all, it will be a lot easier to meet in cyberspace. And second, if you did meet face-to-face, the person would find out that you weren't really the virtual Adonis that she had been talking to in the virtual world.

> *Any smoothly functioning technology will have the appearance of magic.*
> —*Arthur C. Clarke*

So clearly, in VR, one of the problems we're going to face is trying to distinguish between what is real and what is pure deception. And this could be a real problem. What, for example, would you do if someone decided to take on your virtual persona for a trip into cyberspace? Suddenly, there is a "virtual you" out there, doing whatever the person wants, without any consideration for how it might reflect on you. You may even meet yourself "out there" one day.

VIRTUAL MORALITY

And what about morality? It's hard not to imagine a complete breakdown of morality in a virtual world. After all, why worry about morality in a world without consequences? The virtual extramarital affair is the classic example. Let's say your husband or wife, in virtual reality, takes on another identity and has a virtual sexual relationship with another virtual being. Would that be wrong? Would that be grounds for divorce? What about a virtual divorce? Well, as you can see, in this area there are more questions than answers. But this situation clearly demonstrates that the virtual world isn't going to be a world without consequences. Just ask the husband whose wife finds him in a virtual hotel room with a virtual hooker. We think the consequences for that guy are going to be quite real.

Basically, it comes down to what is real and what is not. In virtual reality, is there also something called virtual virtue? How about virtual truth, virtual love, or virtual fidelity? And how will this change as VR becomes every bit as real as reality itself?

WHERE IS VR GOING FROM HERE?

As in the case of any technology, it's a whole lot harder to predict where it will go in the future than it is to talk about its impact in the present. In the case of VR, however, some future courses can be considered pretty much inevitable. The first of these, and perhaps the most talked about (and also the most obvious), is the world of virtual sex.

SEX WITH A COMPUTER? ABSOLUTELY!

It's pretty obvious to anyone studying virtual reality that with all the recent advances in this area, and the even greater advances waiting in the wings, the fiercely competitive selling of sex cannot be far behind. The obvious question that springs to the mind of any reasonable person is, of course, "What? Sex with a machine?" Unfortunately, the answer is a resounding "Absolutely!"

If you want to know how big a role sex is going to play in cyberspace in the future, take a look at it in the present. A good place to start is in a part of the Internet world known as the UseNet. The UseNet is a vast collection of newsgroups, where people from literally every corner of the planet can come together in a text-based world to discuss various subjects and exchange computer files.

SOMETHING FOR EVERYONE

The newsgroups have names as varied as alt.business.internal.audit; alt.clothes.designer; alt.-tv.baywatch; and misc.forsale.computers. For the Christian there are dozens of discussion groups, including alt.bible.prophecy and alt.religion.christian. The number of such groups is expanding almost as fast as the universe, numbering at any one time in the tens of thousands. And that's really not surprising, given the diversity of interests in the world. No subject is too small to have its own newsgroup when you are talking about millions and millions of people around the world. In other words, no matter what you're interested in, with that kind of a population to work with, you're bound to find someone to talk to about it. Hence the existence of such groups as alt.fan.barry.manilow; alt.food.taco.bell; and alt.-lifestyle.barefoot. You know that if you can find someone who has nothing better to do than to talk about the food at Taco Bell, then you've tapped into a pretty sizable (and bored) population.

SEX ON THE NET

When it comes to the world of sex on the Internet, however, you're not going to have any trouble at all finding people to talk to. And a lot more than talking is going on. Every day, pornography is posted for anyone with a computer to see, rendezvous are arranged, and sex is for sale in dozens of newsgroups. Here you will find the greatest activity anywhere on the UseNet. With names such as ....sex.pictures, ...sex.spanking, and ....picture.erotica, it should come as no surprise that when the newsgroups are listed, ranked by popularity, the sex groups generally account for numbers 1, 2, 3, 4, 5, 6, 7, 8, 9, and 10.

And just who is spending all this time on the Internet, gawking at pictures of other people having sex? Well, no question about it, kids are among the big users. After all, it's a lot easier, cheaper, and certainly less embarrassing than trying to buy pornography at the corner store. And unless parents have taken rather complex steps to prevent their children from accessing these sites, then there's really nothing standing in the way. Look in any sexually oriented newsgroup and you'll see messages with titles such as, "How do I hide porno pictures on my computer so my parents won't find them?"

But kids certainly aren't the only audience for this stuff. Other, even more troubling newsgroups exist, including ....sex.sleeping.girls, ...sex.pedophila, and ....sex.children. Sex with a machine? Absolutely!

WHAT A TANGLED WEB WE WEAVE

What about the rest of the Internet? What about the good old World Wide Web that we hear so much about? Well, again, sex is not only king of the newsgroups, but it's king of the Web too. The top sites, according to most surveys, include *Playboy* and *Penthouse* magazine pages, and a host of other lesser known pornography sites. It took only a few minutes to find sites with names such as VR Sex Live, CyberLust, and Porn Palace. One of them even had the phrase "Porn is great. Porn is good" scrolling across the bottom of the screen!

Many of the sites offer a wide selection of pornographic pictures, much like the ones found in the UseNet newsgroups. But on the Web there is another option not available in the UseNet. It's live sex, and it is spreading across the Web like a bad rash (pardon the pun). When you visit a live sex site, you can experience a private sex show (for a price, of course) with a live model. If you're not too shy, you can even talk to her through the microphone included with most new computers. She can talk back through your PC speakers, so it's almost like being in the same room. You can sit back and instruct her to do whatever you like, and watch it all happening on your computer screen. Most observers believe that these could become the most popular sites on the entire World Wide Web. One such site proudly boasted, "60,564 visitors in the last 7 days"!

But surely, these sites must have some line of defense to keep their adult images away from curious young eyes, right? Wrong. In reality, the only line of defense is the parents of the kids using the computers. Although some sites can be blocked using home-censoring software, most can't, and the only foolproof way that parents have of keeping their children safe from such smut is to sit there right beside them while they surf the Net. For now, however, our point is this: Electronic sex is here to stay.

REACH OUT AND TOUCH SOMEONE

What does all this have to do with the future of virtual reality? You've probably guessed already. Sex is big business in this world, and few observers have any doubt that sex is also going to drive the development of VR. Imagine the possibilities for sex in virtual reality. In a full bodysuit participants could receive sensations wherever their virtual partners touch them. It becomes a two-way street instead of the passive-observer approach of the Internet.

And the interactive element of VR sex is going to be a very powerful addition to traditional pornography. Just look at the number of 900 sex lines advertised on TV late at night. Here we have no images whatsoever, just audio, and yet this has exploded into a multimillion-dollar industry. Imagine the power of combining all of these elements, sight, sound, and touch!

Besides the obvious moral decay that such a world represents, there are other problems too. In the world of virtual sex, you can have any partner you want. A movie star, a neighbor, a teacher, a secretary, even a child. Any fantasy can be played out in full, without the risk of consequences. But obviously, there are consequences in the *real* world, even if there aren't in the *virtual* world.

No Holds Barred

Consider, for example, what happens to the mind of a man who has been sleeping with his neighbor's wife in virtual reality for three and a half years. Can he interact with her in the real world the same way he always has? Won't the temptation be all that much greater than it would have been without VR, and won't the barriers holding him back be somewhat broken down? After all, they've already made love hundreds of times. And don't forget, in this virtual world she was a willing accomplice who wanted him as much as he wanted her.

And what about a scenario where she resists his advances at first, even physically fighting against him? Then after he overpowers her resistance, she succumbs, telling him that she's always loved him more than she loves her husband, and that she's glad he pushed her to do what she really wanted all along. Back in the real world, her true resistance may now seem to him to be just part of the fantasy. He may truly believe that her resistance is merely temporary, and that it's only a matter of time until she lets her conscience go and follows her passion. It's a pretty scary picture, that's for sure.

And what about the woman's husband? The VR world can be a complicated one. How would you feel if you found out that your neighbor had a virtual reality computer system in his house, and that every night, in his own VR world, he was sleeping with your wife? Or even worse, what if he was fantasizing about having sex with your ten-year-old son or daughter? Even though nothing had actually taken place in the real world, wouldn't you feel terribly threatened and angry anyway? And wouldn't you somehow feel that your rights had been violated?

THE SLIPPERY SLOPE OF FANTASY AND VIOLENCE

Another reasonable concern would be the old issue of fantasy leading to reality. Many carefully controlled studies done in the 1980s demonstrated that children who were exposed to violent behavior (zapping bad guys) in video games, played much more aggressively afterward than children who played more passive games, such as solitaire or chess. Now think about the video games that were available in the 1980s. Poor graphics, unrealistic "enemies," and an overall cartoonish effect certainly took away from the realism of the game.

But today, and even more so tomorrow, the games are hundreds of times more realistic. Add to that the VR equipment and the feeling of actually "being there," and the potency is increased even more. Imagine once again little Johnny coming home after school and blowing his teacher's head off with a virtual shotgun.

To think that such behavior, especially when repeated over an extended period of time, is not going to have an effect on Johnny's life in the real world is more than a little naive. Overall, we have to worry about desensitization. How much easier it is to repeat an act for the twentieth time than it is to do it for the first time. In VR, you can get that experience in a "safe" world before taking it outside for the greatest thrill of all.

VR: THE NEXT GENERATION

As so often seems to be the case, we can look to Hollywood for a portrayal of just how far "out there" the limits of science may be. And rest assured, Hollywood has not let us down in the area of virtual reality. Movies such as *Total Recall, Lawnmower Man,* and *The Ghost in the Machine* have certainly helped to increase interest in virtual reality, and have also painted a picture of where technology may take us in the future.

But perhaps the best portrayal of the ultimate virtual reality world is found in the television series *Star Trek: The Next Generation.* On board the starship *Enterprise* is a wonderful place known as the holodeck. The holodeck is a room that allows you to walk into a computer-generated environment that is, quite literally, indistinguishable from reality. In the holodeck you can pick up objects, interact with people, skydive, scuba dive, sword fight, fist fight, or play poker with Abraham Lincoln and Richard Nixon at the same time. Anything you can imagine, you can have in the holodeck.

Of course, the holodeck is pure science fiction, and just how far we are from achieving it is an issue of hot debate among VR experts. But no matter how near or far it may be, one thing is certain. That holodeck is serving a huge role in driving the research farther and faster. It is the level of VR to which everyone aspires.

Although a few episodes in the *Star Trek* series deal with the obvious issue, it is generally not a matter of concern for the crew of the USS *Enterprise.* The issue is addiction. If we're spending an average of seven hours a day in front of the TV, then imagine how much time you'd spend in the holodeck if you had one. We've worked hard on some rough calculations and determined that it would be approximately 100 percent of your time, assuming that you could look after your basic bodily functions without having to exit your perfect world.

DECEPTION: IT'S A VIRTUAL REALITY

The spiritual implications of VR are staggering. Think about being able to use your computer to create any environment you want. It's like being able to create your own world. You can choose the setting, the climate, the people and even how those people will respond to you.

But if you can choose every detail of that world, aren't you the god of that world? You could even have every person you came into contact with bow down and worship you. Why not? It's your world.

You know, the promise of godhood has always been at the heart of Satan's lie to humankind. But today, with the advent of virtual reality we'll be able to hear the promise, and we'll be able to taste the fruit.

Isn't it amazing that the very generation that has witnessed Israel coming back into her land, has seen knowledge literally explode, and is now anxiously awaiting its first contact is also the same generation that is able to get a taste of godhood through virtual reality?

RACING TOWARD THE IMAGE OF THE BEAST

But that's not the only spiritual implication of VR. There is one specific prophecy that we don't believe has ever been understood until now. It is the prophecy of the image of the Beast spoken by the apostle John. Speaking of the False Prophet, who will rule alongside the Antichrist, or Beast as John called him, he foresaw something that has been wrapped in a mystery for two thousand years:

> And [he] deceiveth them that dwell on the earth by the means of those miracles which he had power to do in the sight of the beast; saying to them that dwell on the earth, that they should make an image to the beast, which had the wound by a sword, and did live. And he had power to give life unto the image of the beast, that the image of the beast should both speak, and cause that as many as would not worship the image of the beast should be killed. (Rev. 13:14–15)

What a remarkable prophecy! Don't forget that John was foreseeing a day when the entire globe will be united into a new world order. People from all over the world will have come together in adoration and worship of the Beast.

> The promise of godhood has always been at the heart of Satan's lie to humankind. But today, with the advent of virtual reality we'll be able to hear the promise, and we'll be able to taste the fruit.
>
> —*Peter Lalonde*

So now the False Prophet declares that the world should make an image to the Beast. But this is no stone statue. It is an image that comes to life and that can speak.

Well, let's consider this very high-tech image for just a second. First of all, the whole world has to be able to worship it, right? So, where are you going to put it? In Paris, New York, or Rome? How are people from South Africa, New Zealand, or China going to get to any of these places to worship it?

No, the whole world has to have access to this image. Well, maybe it could be on TV, you might say. That solves half of the problem. Now you can see the Beast in the privacy of your own home. But TV provides for only one-way communication. How will the powers that be know whether you are worshiping it or not?

THE BEAST FROM CYBERSPACE

Consider, however, the possibility that the image of the Beast may not really exist in our natural, physical world. What if this image existed only in cyberspace? For one thing it would get rid of the problem of where to put up this image. Everyone on the planet will soon have access to cyberspace, and remember the words of William Gibson, in that world "there is no there, there."

Moreover, the second generation of VR systems will allow more than one real person to share the same virtual world. Indeed, like our Thanksgiving dinner story, when the speed of the Internet increases to the levels it will in the next few years, you could have two or three million people sharing the same virtual world.

So what if this is where the image is? Now we can understand how an image could come to life and even speak. And in such an electronic and interactive world we can even understand how it would be possible for this image to know if you are worshiping it or not.

Of course, we can't be certain how this prophecy will be fulfilled, but one thing is certain. Some intriguing possibilities exist today that we could not have understood in any other generation.

CHAPTER 7

The future ain't what it used to be.
—*Arthur C. Clarke*

THE FUTURE: WHERE WE'LL SPEND THE REST OF OUR LIVES

We've talked a lot about technology in this book, and we're sure you'll agree with us that the breakthroughs we have already seen in this generation are nothing short of phenomenal. However, some other new thought-provoking developments are also going to be coming into our lives in the very near future. And since the future is where all of us will be spending the rest of our lives, we thought we'd take a few minutes to give you a peek at what may be waiting for us around the very next corner.

First of all, we want to make one thing perfectly clear. This chapter is not about predicting the future. We believe that the Lord could come back at any moment, and that would, of course, change everything. And assuming that He does not return right away, we are still not going to speculate about what incredible breakthroughs may come in the next century. Breakthroughs make the future hard to predict, and to see how true that is, we need look only to the past.

Consider electronics, for example, an area of technology that may be the most important breakthrough to come along since the industrial revolution. Barely more than a hundred years ago, the electron simply did not exist in the minds of people. Therefore, imagining the electronic future was impossible, and things such as electronic televisions and computers weren't even imagined.

TRENDS VS. BREAKTHROUGHS

Today, in many ways, we find ourselves in a similar position. While it may be possible to forecast trends and developments within specific industries, it is quite another matter to try to predict bona fide breakthroughs. And because the great breakthrough discoveries can set so many new things into motion, they can have a truly paradigm-shifting effect. The printing press, the automobile, the television, the telephone, the computer— these breakthroughs had such an enormous effect on society that they literally changed the very nature of the way we live our lives.

So, for the remainder of this chapter, we're not going to try to predict what things might be like in the unforeseeable future. Instead, we're going to talk about trends that are already in motion. We're going to look at some of the most promising new technologies awaiting us. Some of them are still being developed, some of them are ready and waiting for commercial viability, and others are waiting for people to be ready to accept them. In each case, though, we are talking about the *real* future, not the *possible* future.

Also, we've not tried to look at all of the trends in the world today. We've specifically focused on the future of technologies that will have the ability to change our understanding of the universe and our place in it. Just as we've talked about how a seeming contact with an outside world could change our fundamental beliefs, or how VR can change our perception of reality, some new technologies could also change our views of life, existence, and even creation. In reporting about one of those technologies, artificial intelligence, *Time* magazine noted that the reality of thinking computers requires "us to stretch our notions of what human thought really is." The special issue entitled "Can Machines Think?" concluded by quoting computer theorist Tom Ray who claims that we now "need to be prepared for an intelligence that is very different from our own."

THINKING COMPUTERS

Whenever you strike up a conversation with people about what life might be like in the future and where technology might take us next, you're bound to hear someone talk about computers with humanlike intelligence.

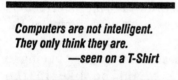

*Computers are not intelligent.
They only think they are.*
—seen on a T-Shirt

A recent poll of American adults found that more than half of those surveyed believed that in the next century, computers will be "as smart as humans and have personalities like humans." Do you think the fact that half of Americans hold this belief has anything to do with the power of today's mass media? Do you think that the representations of the future presented by Hollywood might have played a role in this unbelievable optimism in the power of technology?

Think again about the ever-popular television series (and the spin-off movies that have made millions and millions of dollars) *Star Trek: The Next Generation*. The officer who is third in command of the starship *Enterprise*, Lieutenant Commander Data, is actually a computer who is apparently "just as smart as humans." In many ways he is much smarter than his human counterparts. Does he have a personality? Absolutely.

The possibility that the public's perceptions about what might be possible in the future were affected by Mr. Data and other futuristic portrayals of intelligent, humanlike computers is certainly a real one. But expectations and Hollywood hype aside, how much truth might there be behind this whole computers-as-smart-as-people situation? To answer that question, let's take a look at the world of artificial intelligence.

WHAT IS AI?

Webster's Dictionary defines AI as "the characteristics of a machine programmed to imitate human intelligence functions." In other words, it is just what its name implies, a machine that thinks. To help in their studies of AI, scientists use something called the Turing Test to evaluate new efforts. According to that test, a computer program can be considered "intelligent" if a person interacting with it is unable to tell whether or not she is dealing with a real person. And the research and development are a lot farther along than you might think, with huge new steps being taken almost every day.

WHY ALL THE INTEREST IN ARTIFICIAL INTELLIGENCE?

Right now, when most people talk about the research going on in the field of AI, they talk about all the ways that artificially intelligent machines could make our lives easier. And who's going to argue with that? After all, our homes and lives are already full of machines designed to ease the burden of everyday life.

It's hard to imagine going through life without televisions, telephones, fax machines, washing machines, cars, planes, and those little things on your refrigerator door that dispense fresh ice cubes.

Adding an element of technological sophistication to any of these devices can only be considered a good thing in the eyes of most people. Imagine a telephone that can decide on its own how to deal with an inbound call. Imagine a washing machine that can sort the colors and whites for you, and that never loses a sock. Imagine a

> *Artificial intelligence: the art of making computers that behave like the ones in the movies.*
> *—Bill Bulko*

television system that automatically videotapes a program that it thinks you might be interested in. That sounds tempting to most people. For some, however, it is a little bit frightening. I

am referring to those millions of people whose VCR's are blinking right now on 12:00. "More electronic gadgetry? No way! I can't even figure out the ones I have." But the truth is that artificially intelligent appliances may have the most appeal to those very people.

SURE MY VCR CAN RECORD PROGRAMS, BUT I CAN'T

Because of the added element of intelligence to some of these everyday gadgets in our lives, the need for our interaction will become less and less. Take the example of videotaping programs from your TV. Right now, even with the very best VCR's that money can buy, setting a VCR to tape several shows over a weekend can be a real challenge. First of all, and this is where most people get hung up, you have to remember to do it. For every person who actually tapes a show using the timer, there are probably ten who say, "Oh, I wanted to tape that, but I forgot."

Second, as we've alluded to before, you can't really set the timer to tape at 6:30 P.M. if your VCR thinks it's 12:00 all the time. Let's say you do remember that you want to set the VCR, and you do manage to get the whole thing set up properly. The toughest task of all is having to scour the entire TV guide from front to back, just to make sure you don't miss a show that you're interested in.

It's an easy thing to say, "I want to tape *This Week in Bible Prophecy* every Thursday night at 7:30 P.M. on TBN." But what about the special on *The Search for Noah's Ark* that's on channel 83 at 4:30 A.M. next Tuesday? Or a show called *The Garden* that's on tonight? Is it about growing vegetables? Is it about the Garden of Eden? Is it a movie about an older man who has nothing left in life but his little flower garden on the roof of his building? Maybe it's the story of Madison Square Garden, the sports arena in New York City. This is where AI technology really starts to sound pretty wonderful.

DON'T WORRY; MY COMPUTER WILL HANDLE IT

Right now, much of AI research is dedicated to the development of something called software agents. In a nutshell, agents are computer programs that "know" enough about their owners to act autonomously on their behalf. And most important, by acting largely on their own, they don't have to bother you with the little details of technology that most people seem to hate.

Imagine having your whole house wired up with intelligent agents. Here is what your morning routine might be like. You wake up at 6:00 to the sound of your alarm, waking you not with a loud buzz, but with the morning weather, top news stories, and maybe your favorite song. You stumble into the bathroom where the shower is already running, adjusted to the temperature you like. You make your way to the closet where your clothes have already been selected, based not only on what you have planned for the day, but also on the latest weather forecast. In the kitchen, the coffee is ready, the toast is just popping up as you walk into the room, and your morning news summary is on the TV. Not the same news summary as your neighbor is getting, but your very own, tailored to your specific interests.

When you go outside to your car, the engine is running, and the electronic dashboard greets you with your agenda for the day. Imagine your car saying, "Good morning, don't forget to pick up the spare key on the way into the office this morning. John called this morning to remind you, but I didn't want to wake you up, and since it wasn't urgent that he talk to you, I simply took a message. And by the way, you don't have enough gas to get all the way to work and back, and since it's always busier on the way home, you might want to stop on the way to work and fill up. There is no lineup at Fifth and Main this morning. I suggest we go there."

This may sound a little futuristic, but in reality all of the technology to make this scenario possible already exists. And it's only a matter of time (a very short time actually) before we see it in our everyday lives. But the most important aspect of these smart agents is not that they can carry out simple tasks on your behalf. Rather, it is that they can learn from experience and get to know your routine by "watching" what you do every day.

COMPUTER, MAKE ME SOME TOAST

A significant development in the computer world is going to be in the area of voice recognition technology. A lot of work is being done in this area, largely because of the enormous commercial possibilities once it succeeds fully. Think about it. A computer that can respond to your voice commands and answer you in perfect English. And you won't have to be a computer whiz to operate the computers of the future. You won't have to know anything about computers at all.

Right now, it is possible to watch TV on your computer. It is possible to program your VCR to tape your favorite program while you're at work. But a very small minority of people do either of these things. Why? "It's too much of a pain" is the most common answer. But how different would life be if all you had to do was say to your television set "Tape *This Week in Bible Prophecy* next Thursday night"? You could ask your computer, "What's the earliest flight I can get to New York tomorrow morning?" Once we cross the voice command barrier in the computer world, the computer will sweep the nation faster than the telephone or television could ever have dreamed of.

PARLEZ-VOUS FRANCAIS? NO, BUT MY COMPUTER DOES!

Another critical development is going to come along hand in hand with the voice recognition technology. You see, once computers are able to recognize our voices, they'll quickly be taught to do something else too—real-time translations.

You'll be able to speak into your computer in English, and your message will come out of a computer in Jerusalem in Hebrew. This capability will truly unite the world, allowing anyone, anywhere, to communicate with anyone else, anywhere else, anytime he wants to. God's division of human language at the tower of Babel will have been reversed, and the world will have been united, at least in language.

> *Time flies like an arrow.*
> *Fruit flies like a banana.*
> *—Example of why it is difficult to get computers to understand human speech*

Now that we have some idea of how AI is being used and developed today, let's turn our attention to the future. Not the distant future of science fiction, but the immediate future, here in our generation of rapid change and high expectations.

MR. DATA, WHERE ARE YOU?

As great as all this AI stuff might sound, there is obviously something missing from the traditional American vision of the future. We're still talking about computers, and a computer, whether it's sitting on your desk or mounted in the dash of your car, is still nothing like a human being.

Imagine taking all of the best aspects of the AI technology discussed so far, and wrapping them all together into a marvelous new package. One of the most talked about packages is the robot, and for most people, the more closely a robot resembles a human being, the better. For years we have seen robots in science fiction movies and on TV shows. And over the past thirty years or so, we have seen them evolve from crude mechanical-sounding machines with lots of flashing lights to robots barely distinguishable from real people.

Today, while the robots in the labs around the country are barely learning to walk, the glamorized androids and artificial life-forms of movies and television have prepared the world to believe that much more sophisticated mechanical beings are not only possible, but also inevitable. And the expectations that Hollywood has fueled are considerable. Perhaps the most famous of all is the robot C-3PO from the *Star Wars* movies. This lovable character looked like a person wearing a gold suit of armor and was not only able to navigate a spaceship, but was also able to experience emotions, most notably fear.

Later, *Star Trek: The Next Generation* came to television screens around the world and with it came Mr. Data, the ultimate artificial life-form. Played by a human actor with lots of makeup to give him a pasty complexion, Mr. Data represents what most people would consider to be the pinnacle of both AI and robotics research. A fully autonomous being, Mr. Data was third in command on the starship *Enterprise*, and when he had his "emotion chip" installed, he was basically indistinguishable from a real human being. He was much stronger and much smarter, and since he was made entirely of replaceable artificial components, he was immortal too.

Mr. Data may be pure science fiction today, but many things that we now take for granted were pure science fiction not very many years ago. And with the pace of change and acceleration of knowledge in this generation, nothing seems to be out of our reach anymore.

Even though there are more than 68,000 robots at work in the United States today (and more than 400,000 in Japan!), they work in manufacturing, especially in automobile factories, and the robots bear very little resemblance to the Hollywood varieties with which most of us are quite familiar. These robots do little more than spot welding, screw turning, and other mundane tasks. Interestingly enough, the word *robot* actually comes from the Czech word *robota*, which means "compulsory labor." But despite these somewhat humble beginnings (compared to Hollywood's robots anyway), the future of robotics promises to be a fascinating one, and the potential for combining the latest developments in artificial intelligence with more sophisticated robots is incredible.

Today, most of the work in the field of artificial intelligence can be broken down into one of two general approaches. The first approach is to create a computer "brain" filled with all the accumulated knowledge of the world. The hope in this research is that eventually the computer will have enough knowledge and know-how to begin seeking out and learning information on its own.

The second approach is somewhat more human in nature, with the computer starting out with very little in the way of a knowledge base, but "learning" every day through interactions with people and other aspects of the environment.

Whichever approach you're talking about, there is still a lot of work to do before we see anything like Mr. Data or C-3PO walking down the street or driving a bus. Again, however, we have to stress that in the world of deception (a key element in the last days scenario) what is plausible is just as important as what is possible. And frankly, if scientists were to hold a press conference tomorrow announcing the development of a thinking, speaking, human-looking robot, the world would eat it up. Hook, line, and sinker.

Speaking of human-looking, that is bound to be another area of research in the days ahead. Even if we could make robots that could act more or less like people, how in the world would we go about making them look like us? No problem!

THE WORLD OF ANIMATRONICS

Animatronics is a relatively new field, but already achievements in this area have been absolutely mind-boggling. Animatronics refers to the use of mechanical and electrical components to simulate a living creature, real or imagined. Obviously, the most common use for such technology comes from Hollywood. In the movie *Operation Dumbo Drop*, a very life like elephant was created for some of the stunts in the movie. The elephant could move just like the real animal, and moviegoers had no idea that a mechanical stand-in was being used. In the movie *Jaws*, it was a mechanical shark, in *The Santa Claus*, mechanical reindeer, and in *Hocus Pocus*, it was a mechanical stand-in for actress Sarah Jessica Parker.

But while Hollywood is one thing, the real world is another thing altogether. Would it really be possible in the future to create artificial human beings that are indistinguishable from the real thing? Absolutely. Rick

Lazzarini, one of Hollywood's leading animatronics artists, has been commissioned by EndoCare, a Los Angeles-based surgery center, to create replicas of human organs for surgeons to practice on before putting the knife to real people. And these are not just approximations. The models must be exact, not only in appearance, but in texture too. Each organ has a different feel against the scalpel, sutures, and scissors, and the models must duplicate those sensations exactly. Dr. Edward Phillips, director of endoscopic surgery at Cedars-Sinai Medical Center, said, "When you put your endoscope inside that model, it really looks like the real thing. It absolutely replaces the need to use animals (for practice surgery)."

IT'S ALIVE! IT'S ALIVE!

It should come as no real surprise to believers in God's creation that the greatest computer ever developed is the one between our ears. But did you know that the fundamental building blocks used by our Creator are now being used in laboratories around the world in an effort to develop computers that will make the greatest computers of today look like pocket calculators in comparison? That's right. Scientists are now working with biological material, DNA, trying to apply its complex principles to the world of computers. If they succeed, we will see unbelievable advances in the area of computing.

While DNA computers are a long way from being considered "life," there is little doubt that the world's imaginations will be set free by any breakthroughs in this area, and our beliefs about what is possible in terms of creating "computers as smart as humans" will be set free.

OUR IMAGE OF THE FUTURE

In our discussion of virtual reality we pointed out how a virtual image of the Beast may be the most likely way in which the apostle John's prophecy will find its fulfillment.

But the prophecy of the image of the Beast could also be fulfilled by these remarkable developments in the world of artificial intelligence and robotics. After all, the prophecy calls for an image that "lives" and "speaks." And as we noted, computer theorist Tom Ray warns that with our existing technologies, we already "need to be prepared for an intelligence that is very different from our own." So, an artificially intelligent image should also be considered when we speak of the image of the Beast.

Beyond that specific prophecy, though, there are wider implications of AI. What if we can *seem* to create intelligent life? Once again, for the purposes of influencing society the big issue is not whether it really has been created; it is whether people believe it has been created.

Like UFO's and VR, artificial intelligence has the ability to get humankind to accept a totally new view of reality, life, our origins, and our future. Isn't it amazing that once again it's all happening in the very generation that saw Israel return to her land—the very generation in which the Bible said that humankind would be led into global confusion and deception?

GET
SET

_____
_____
_____
_____
_____
_____
_____
_____
_____
_____
_____
_____
_____
_____
_____
_____
_____
_____

CHAPTER  8   *The new electronic interdependence re-creates the
world in the image of a global village.*
—*Marshall McLuhan*

FRONT ROW SEATS!

Imagine if the Lord had returned in 1809. That would mean that all of the prophecies surrounding His return would have been fulfilled before then. And try to imagine yourself, as a believer, living in Niagara Falls three years earlier in 1806.

The prophecies would have been different because the Lord would have prophesied what the world would be like in that day, not this one. Nonetheless, you would have been living in the moment when major end-time prophecies were being fulfilled, right?

So how would you know about it? How could you track all of these various fulfillments of prophecy to determine that you were indeed living in the last days? With any luck you might get the latest news from Europe within a month or so. Or maybe your neighbor would get a letter from a family member with a bit of gossip from Asia that he could tell you about when he came to trade some cheese for a beaver pelt.

HAVE YOU EVER HEARD OF TONYA HARDING?

The point is that today we live in the first generation where it is possible for Christians to track world events and make the determination that prophecy is indeed being fulfilled. All we have to do is sit down with a Bible, flip on CNN, and we can watch it all happen right before our very eyes. We don't even have to wait for tomorrow's newspaper to get today's news. We can watch it live.

Together, as a global community, we watched the Berlin Wall coming down—live. We saw Tonya Harding skate for gold against Nancy Kerrigan—live. And we even watched a war, the Gulf War, in real time.

A HIDDEN PROPHECY

Jesus gave the disciples a list of dozens of prophecies when they asked Him what would be the sign of His second coming. Then He said something that has been completely overlooked as a prophecy, but that we believe is a key one. He said, "When these things begin to come to pass, then look up, and lift up your heads; for your redemption draweth nigh" (Luke 21:28).

This is the first generation that can see those things begin to come to pass. We live in Niagara Falls, Canada. Neither we nor our wives have seen an earthquake, for example. Yet Jesus said that an increase in earthquakes

> *If it weren't for Philo T. Farnsworth, inventor of television, we'd still be eating frozen radio dinners.*
> *— Johnny Carson*

would be one of the things to watch for to show that His coming was near.

Today, however, we don't have to feel earthquakes to know they are on the rise. We see them happening, or the results of them happening, almost every night on the news. We remember watching the San Francisco quake in the late 1980s. Though we were thousands of miles away, we felt as if we were a part of it as we, along with the rest of the continent, watched live coverage.

The same thing is true with the violent storms, wars, or battles over Jerusalem's Temple Mount. We can watch it all happen from the comfort of our living rooms. What a unique and awesome time to be alive! What a time for prophecy to be fulfilled—when people can see it with their own eyes!

Sometimes it's easy to take things for granted. For example, neither of us has ever had to commute to the office in a horse and buggy. We use the car without giving it a second thought. That is, until the car is in the shop, and our lives fall into complete chaos. That is like so much of our world today, but if we can step back and try to look at this world through the eyes of someone who lived in say the 1800s, we'll see things such as today's mass media as integral parts of Bible prophecy in a way that we never have before.

THE MOST OVERLOOKED PIECE OF THE PROPHETIC PUZZLE

We believe that the emergence of the global mass media is one of the most significant and overlooked prophetic developments of our generation. Like the explosion of knowledge, the birth of virtual reality, and the influence of science fiction, the emergence of a global mass media makes possible prophecies that could never before have been fulfilled.

And the mass media may even be more significant because, almost all of our knowledge about those other areas comes through this worldwide communication system.

A moment ago we talked about the fact that you could not have seen the myriad of prophetic fulfillments in any other generation because there was no reliable way to get the information transmitted to you. But as you carefully study Bible prophecy, it becomes clear that today's media are not only necessary to report on prophetic fulfillments, they are also necessary to fulfill prophecy in and of itself.

THE ANTICHRIST ON EYEWITNESS NEWS

Let's consider, for example, the rise of the Antichrist onto the world scene in the last days. The apostle John described this coming dictator in detail in the book of Revelation. In that book we get insights into the titanic battle between God and Satan, but we also get a very practical chronology of the compressed time period known as the Great Tribulation.

John told us that in three and one-half years, the Antichrist sets up a world government and an integrated world economy. He brings all the world's religions, divided forever, into a united single world religion. He establishes a powerful and effective global army. He puts a stop to the conflict in the Middle East and establishes a seven-year treaty that covers not only the Middle East, but the whole world. He has the temple rebuilt in Jerusalem and creates a global electronic identification system that encompasses virtually every man, woman, and child on the planet. And to top it all off, he gets the whole world to worship him as God!

Now, even for the Antichrist—the master of evil and deception—that's a pretty long and involved list. If you think about it, in other generations there was no way everyone on the entire planet could even know who this guy was, never mind worship him as God. But today, ask Tonya Harding, Marcia Clark, or Norman Schwarzkopf how quickly your name can become a household word.

INSTANT COFFEE, INSTANT BREAKFAST, INSTANT REVOLUTION

Through our mass media today, a person, an idea, or both can come to the center stage of the entire world in a few moments. Even a thing like a white Ford Bronco can suddenly become famous and have sales jump through the roof!

How powerful a role do the media play in bringing people and ideas to the forefront of the world's consciousness? Well, consider this. According to Ted Turner, he and his CNN network brought down the Berlin Wall! Now, Ted's not the most modest guy around, but we should not dismiss the significance of his point.

Fueled by the mass media, it is said that the revolution of 1989 took ten years to bear fruit in Poland, ten months to leap across the border to Hungary, ten weeks to germinate in East Germany, ten days to spread like fire in Czechoslovakia, and ten hours to purge a totalitarian leader in Romania.

Asked about the role of Western media in Poland's liberation, Lech Walesa smiled and asked, "Would there be land and earth without a sun?" Likewise, many believe that Israel is being forced into concessions with the Palestinians today because the mass media decided to focus world attention on the stone-throwing tactics of the Intifada. Recently, we interviewed a top Israeli official, Pinhaus Dror. He recounted how the media can not only focus attention but also manipulate the images you see of the world around you:

> I will give you one example. I don't want to badmouth any television crew right now, but years ago a famous TV chain in the United States sent a crew to the West Bank and they bribed, and it was all documented, they bribed a young Arab boy, twelve years old, to put a tire on fire. Now I will tell you if you would put a zoom on a television lens through the smoke, you will make believe that the whole city was on fire, but it was one tire. So the fact that you watch it on television doesn't mean that this is true. You are only watching it on television and what you are seeing is the picture that was staged by the producer, by the cameraman, and they can do

whatever they want. And you make believe that this is true. This is not true. This is the truth that they want you to see.

Is CNN Running American Foreign Policy?

Remember Ted Turner's claim that he and his CNN network brought down the Berlin Wall? As we noted, that's a typical Ted Turner statement. But you can't deny the fact that he who defines the mental boundaries of today does very much set the political, military, and economic boundaries of tomorrow.

So, are there thirteen men in some smoke-filled room determining every piece of news so that they can get us to do exactly what they want? No.

Is news fed to us every day specifically to influence our beliefs and behavior? Absolutely. Everyday press agents plant the news from an angle advantageous to their clients and politicians remake themselves into an image that will be most desirable to you.

Moreover, no one can deny that there is a definite liberal bias in our media today. And no one with a brain in his head can fail to see how the media affect the choices we make on the political front either.

For example, policy makers in the United States today worry about what they call the CNN curve. That is when CNN floods the airwaves with a particular news story, politicians have virtually no choice but to redirect their attention to the crisis that CNN has chosen for them. Many worry that this has made CNN the sixth vote on the United Nations Security Council.

If CNN has indeed become a driving force in setting foreign policy, it brings with it the baggage of television—a short attention span that can take you around the world in thirty minutes. As Secretary of State Madeleine Albright testified to the Foreign Relations Committee:

Television's ability to bring graphic images of pain and
outrage into our living rooms has heightened the pressure
both for immediate engagement in areas of international
crisis and immediate disengagement when events do not go
according to plan.

So, there is little doubt that in addition to influencing
society in regard to the importance of owning the Jaclyn
Smith Kmart Collection, or influencing our beliefs on
abortion, welfare, or immigration policy, the media
actually set the specific foreign policy issues of the day.

The point is this. Today's media can incite rapid and
dramatic change unlike anything in history. The media can
elevate someone to power very, very quickly. But to
suggest that there is an orchestrated plot to manage every
bit of news and information in our world is just taking it
too far. That does not, however, mean that the day is not
coming when the media will play such a role. Read the
passages from the book of Revelation once again where
the apostle John described a day when the whole world
will become as one and "wonder after" the beast and even
"worship" him. It will be the day when the power of this
false christ and his perfect exploitation of media images
will truly and finally make the world of "one mind."

Today, the world may complain of a lack of leadership.
But imagine tomorrow when the most deceptive and
powerful leader this world has ever known takes the stage
with the power of a global media at his disposal.

THIS JUST IN . . . YOU'VE BEEN LEFT BEHIND

As we've read the writings of men and women of God
from years gone by who were trying to understand the
prophecies of the Bible, we can now see that one of the
key things they could not foresee was television. That
piece of the puzzle remained a mystery until our very day.
But it is such a central and critical piece of the puzzle that

it may not be going too far to say that this "window on the world" is quite possibly the most powerful and influential force on the planet.

When we were writing the screenplay for our video *Left Behind*, we faced a real dilemma. The video opens with a Hollywood-like enactment of the world in the moments following the rapture. But how could we even begin to imagine what would be happening in a world where millions of people had just vanished?

Then it struck us. We knew exactly how to begin the action because we knew what people would be doing in the moment following the rapture. So, the video opens with a man running into his house and turning on his television set. There is no doubt in our minds that in our world today, that is where everyone will be heading for answers.

HOW'S THAT FOR AN ENTRANCE?

Think of that scene. Millions of men, women, and children will have vanished off the face of the earth. People will be in a state of panic and confusion. Many, if not most, will be at the brink of insanity.

People will clearly recognize that something out of this world has happened. We believe that very few will be disappointed that they have been left behind. Instead, most will thank their lucky stars that they were spared. They won't believe for one second that it was an event in which God took those who believed into the heavens to be with Him. Actually, they will believe anything else—most likely that the world has been attacked by aliens.

Into this powerfully charged, worldwide moment, the Bible tells us, the most powerful and deceptive leader the world has ever known steps onto the world stage. What a moment for the one who comes "with all power and signs and lying wonders"! (2 Thess. 2:9). What a scenario for a deception. It will be so powerful that Jesus warned, if it were possible, even the very elect would be deceived.

Through today's worldwide television links, this entrance will gain its full and unadulterated power. It may not be too much to say that the name of this great leader will be on the lips of every world citizen within twenty-four hours of the rapture.

Your TV Guide to Revelation 13

The thirteenth chapter of the book of Revelation is one of the most remarkable prophetic chapters in the Bible. Within its eighteen short verses we learn of the coming mark of the Beast, the image of the Beast, a worldwide army, and several other key prophetic events.

But take a second with us if you would and try to imagine what the world will be like in the moments following the rapture. Imagine the panic. Imagine the search for answers to this unthinkable event. Picture the television newscasts as reporters scurry to try to file reports from around the globe. Think of the scenes of carnage and destruction. Now imagine this great false christ appearing on those same televisions with a powerful presence, an explanation for what has happened, and the ability to do miracles to prove that he is who he says he is.

In that light, you can't deny how the words of the apostle John, written two thousand years ago, seem to fit this mass media, global age perfectly. He told us that this Antichrist, or Beast as he is also known, will have "a mouth speaking great things" and that he will become the leader of "all kindreds, and tongues, and nations." That all the world will be mesmerized by the Beast. And also that "all that dwell upon the earth shall worship him" (vv. 5, 7, 8).

Once again, how could the entire world have even

heard of this guy, let alone turn the reins of the world over to him, without the power of today's global television systems?

GOD'S PRIME-TIME WITNESSES—A FAR CRY FROM KATO KAELIN!

Now, if that doesn't help you see today's mass media in the book of Revelation, try this one on for size.

The apostle John also told us that once this false leader has gained control of the world, God is going to send two men who will be His two witnesses to the world. These two witnesses will warn of the deception the world is so openly embracing and call the people of the world to repentance. But the people will hate these two witnesses because they will be so devoted to the Antichrist. And when God's witnesses have given their message to the world, the apostle John foresaw that "the beast that ascendeth out of the bottomless pit shall make war against them, and shall overcome them, and kill them." But now discover what John saw happening next:

> And their dead bodies shall lie in the street of the great city, which spiritually is called Sodom and Egypt, where also our Lord was crucified. And they of the people and kindreds and tongues and nations shall see their dead bodies three days and an half, and shall not suffer their dead bodies to be put in graves. And they that dwell upon the earth shall rejoice over them, and make merry, and shall send gifts one to another; because these two prophets tormented them that dwelt on the earth. (Rev. 11:7–10)

What is clear here is that the people of the whole world see this. And they see it within three and one-half days. Obviously, everyone on the planet is not going to travel to Jerusalem. But today, people don't have to. They only have to travel to the family room! And if they stay tuned in, which we know they will, they're about to see something else as well:

> And after three days and an half the spirit of life from God entered into them, and they stood upon their feet; and great fear fell upon them which saw them. And they heard a great voice from heaven saying unto them, Come up hither. And they ascended up to heaven in a cloud; and their enemies beheld them. (Rev. 11:11–12).

EVERY EYE SHALL SEE HIM

One idea that has been suggested is that through television, the world will see Jesus return to earth at the end of the Tribulation: "Behold, he cometh with clouds; and every eye shall see him, and they also which pierced him: and all kindreds of the earth shall wail because of him" (Rev. 1:7).

This is, however, one instance where we don't believe that the media will play any role whatsoever. Television is a medium of deception, illusion, and make-believe. We believe that the Lord will be seen directly by the eye of every person on earth. There will be no chance for people to think that this is some form of illusion or trickery.

Of course, the world is round. How can people on the opposite side of the world see Jesus when He returns to Jerusalem? Since God is God, we think He can handle it!

CHAPTER 9

IT'S NOT AS *THINK* AS YOU *CLEAR* IT IS!

It's three-thirty on a warm summer afternoon. The bus chugs through the city picking up passengers making their way home from another day at the old grind.

At a stop near the end of the line, a man gets on the bus. He looks tired and distant as he trudges up the steps with his backpack. He works his way through all of the other passengers who also got on too late to get a seat. He mumbles apologies and finally finds a spot.

As the bus makes its way into traffic, the young man reaches into his backpack and pulls a cord . . .

> Tel Aviv (AP)—A suicide bomber in Tel Aviv today blew up a rush hour bus killing himself and 62 commuters in retaliation for the latest Israeli initiatives at the Temple Mount in the heart of Jerusalem.

WHAT KIND OF AN IDIOT . . . ?

When we hear of such stories many of us wonder how any man could be persuaded to do such a thing. Imagine pulling a cord that you know will blow you into a million bits. Yet it does happen. How many times have we heard of men giving up their lives for something they so strongly believe in? It may be for a cause that seems noble like defending one's country or saving a child. Or it may seem like nothing more than sheer terrorism. Depending on your particular point of reference, the same single event can be viewed as either heroic or cowardly.

But the point is, people are willing to take very strong action, even to the point of death, for something in which they believe. Those who create the beliefs within a society hold tremendous power.

Men went to Vietnam, for example, because they believed they were defending freedom. For that they were willing to die. When the truth about that war became apparent, many Americans became so outraged that it placed a scar on the nation that has remained to this day.

History has demonstrated the power of belief and guiding images time and time again. If the leader of a tribe can convince his people that another tribe is evil, he can get them to follow him into war. Even in our modern world, Ronald Reagan knew that calling the Soviet Union an "evil empire" would build support for his military budgets. Likewise, Serbs and Muslims in Bosnia seem to have almost unchangeable beliefs that have committed them to destroying the other, even if they wipe themselves out in the process.

From Father to Son to Son to Son

We all know that people have different beliefs and values depending on their personal experience. But entire cultures also differ greatly because of their unique histories and collective experience.

Native Americans passed their traditions on from one generation to another through their stories and accounts of the great battles, the majestic heroes, and the help of the spirits. And traditions are passed from one generation to the next by the Jews through the keeping of holy days and ceremonies—even for those who do not believe.

This culture, or context, in turn has an extensive impact on the beliefs and worldviews of the individuals within the given ethnic group. That's why it is very rare to find a pro-Israeli Palestinian, a pro-English French Canadian, or a pro-Communist American. Thus, it would be fair to say that someone who could control the stories and traditions that brought a culture together would have tremendous influence over the individuals who were a part of the culture.

THE "IDIOT BOX" CULTURE

Where does our culture come from today? Think about it for a moment, and the answer will become obvious. Television fills 80 percent of the leisure time for most North American households. When people are asked who their role models are, who they really wish they could be like, they almost always point to someone on TV. And it's no wonder. It's hard to be as clever in real life as a guy on TV who has a team of sixteen writers planning his every word and action. Imagine how witty you could be with sixteen of the funniest people in America giving you the right line, in advance, of every situation.

Or how can you be as cool as Bruce Willis or Arnold Schwarzenegger, who can jump off a ten-story building, swear for a second, grab an arm, and keep running after the bad guy?

And that's the point. The media heroes of today are the heroes of our culture. They are our examples and the basis of our mythology. Their adventures make up the one thing we all have in common. We can travel to Dallas, Texas, from our homes in Canada and immediately have a conversation with someone about the latest Harrison Ford movie. It's our common point of contact.

Today, we build our definitions of ethnicity or race, and of "us" and "them," out of the images of the media. For example, we have not personally had the opportunity to meet many Hispanic people in our lives. Thus, virtually everything we know about Hispanics comes from television. Think of that power to identify and characterize various groups. And now, think of how that power has been used by the mass media to characterize evangelical Christians.

> I used to think I was poor. Then they told me I wasn't poor, I was needy. Then they told me it was self-defeating to think of myself as needy. I was deprived. (Oh not deprived but rather underprivileged.) Then they told me that underprivileged was overused. I was disadvantaged. I still don't have a dime. But I have a great vocabulary.
> —Jules Feiffer (1965)

YOU ARE WHO WE SAY YOU ARE!

It is not too much to say that the identities of most North Americans are now forged out of the examples found in our mass media. The television and movie industries tell us what it means to be men or women, good guys or bad guys, successes or failures, powerful or impotent. The media define for us our worldviews and what we consider to be important and what is silly or dangerous. And the media stories, as we've said, provide the common symbols and myths upon which a common culture is being forged. As Senator Bill Bradley recently observed:

> At a time when harassed parents spend less time with their children, they've ceded to television more and more the all important role of story telling which is essential to the formation of the moral education that sustains a civil society.

Likewise, David Marc, a writer and observer of popular culture, points out that television creates "a body of dreams that is, to a large extent, the culture we live in. . . . [It is] the most effective purveyor of language, image, and narrative in American culture." And George Gerbner, dean emeritus of the Annenberg School for Communication at the University of Pennsylvania, agrees, "Television provides, perhaps for the first time since preindustrial religion, a strong cultural link, a shared daily ritual of highly compelling and informative content."

In a medium that is highly pleasing to our senses, we cannot deny the power to seduce people into accepting certain views, attitudes, beliefs, and values. Moreover, the lines between fantasy and reality are becoming blurred so that if Frasier Crane says something, it carries great weight because millions of people want to be like Frasier Crane. It doesn't occur to them that Kelsey Grammer, who plays the psychiatrist on the popular NBC series, is actually an actor with a team of writers. One commentator complained of the confusion a few years ago, saying that the problem is that Ed Asner has the image of Lou Grant and mind of Ed Asner.

But today, people such as Kelsey Grammer, Bill Cosby, and Roseanne, along with their writers and studio bosses, hold unparalleled influence in shaping our culture.

SEINFELD VS. ROSEANNE OR CLINTON VS. DOLE?

Imagine that on the night of the presidential debate there was also, on another network, a debate on the issues facing the nation between Jerry Seinfeld and Roseanne. Which do you think would draw the larger audience?

If there is any doubt in your mind, let us remind you that the Smithsonian Institution's exhibit of *Star Trek* has far greater traffic than the *Apollo 11* exhibit. And the O. J. trial received about five thousand times the media coverage of the most recent presidential election.

This point brings up the power of celebrity in our modern-day culture. In past generations someone would gain fame because of a heroic deed, scholarly insight, or political courage. Leading voices in the culture were men or women who had shown great strength or wisdom.

Today, that is no longer the case. As the revealing book *High Visibility* points out, it began to change in the golden days of Hollywood:

> What happened in this period is that the public ceased to insist that there be an obvious correlation between achievement and fame. It was no longer absolutely necessary for its favorites to perform a real life heroic act, to invent a boon for mankind, to create a mighty business enterprise. . . . Beginning with the rise of the star system in Hollywood, it was possible to achieve "celebrity" through attainments in the realm of play—spectator sports, acting— and almost immediately thereafter it became possible to become a celebrity (a new coinage describing a new phenomena) simply by becoming . . . a celebrity.
> (Edited by Erving J. Rien, Philip Kotler, R. Stoller)

We have reached the extreme end of this reality. Celebrity-hood, in and of itself, has become the prize commodity that offers unimaginable riches and power to its possessors. It no longer has anything to do with accomplishment or insight. By and large, what is necessary is money.

The visibility industry, which offers everything from cosmetic surgery to makeovers and from image planning to public speaking lessons, has become one of the largest industries in the world. It is also one of the most secretive. That's because by its very nature it must remain hidden, or its clients would be seen to be nothing more than created images instead of something special.

At the same time, the celebrity creators don't ask if Madonna, Dennis Rodman, and Richard Gere should be as powerful as they are. They are creating a commodity for market. If that celebrity then uses the position to voice certain opinions, that is incidental to their business.

It was interesting recently to watch an edition of the television program *Politically Incorrect* with Bill Maher as host. The subject of the discussion was what role the government should play in our lives. One of the guests was the Libertarian candidate for president. Another was Jason Alexander—George on *Seinfeld*.

Now we could understand what the Libertarian candidate might have to say on the subject. But George? Why was he there? Was it because he was a student of government? No, as it quickly became obvious, he was not. When he was asked for government's greatest contribution, he suggested it must be free condom distribution!

> *It is difficult to produce a television documentary that is both incisive and probing when every twelve minutes one is interrupted by twelve dancing rabbits singing about toilet paper.*
>
> —Rod Serling

Clearly, George was there because he wanted to further his image as funny guy. And he was asked to be there because he is good at playing the role of an unemployed loser on a very funny television program.

We are not saying that Jason Alexander should not have a voice in politics. We are just pointing out the phenomenal power of today's media to give positions of influence to people because they are famous—for whatever, if any, reason.

However, the lessons of the Hollywood celebrity industry have spread far beyond the borders of Tinseltown. Now leading figures in politics, business, and even religion have learned how easily the distinctions between reality and fantasy can be blurred in the minds of an unsuspecting world.

MY FAIR MAYOR

Most of us have seen the wonderful play *Pygmalion* or its movie counterpart, *My Fair Lady*. The famous line "I think she's got it! . . . By George she's got it!" refers to the fact that Henry Higgins, on a wager, has succeeded in transforming a coarse, Cockney girl into a woman who fit right into high society. The movies *Trading Places* with Eddie Murphy and Dan Aykroyd and *Overboard* with Goldie Hawn and Kurt Russell are also Hollywood movies showing how such dramatic transformations can be manufactured.

But in today's world the lessons of Hollywood have spread far beyond the entertainment industry. Lawyers, businesspeople, and politicians are all recognizing the importance of visibility and image management. Greater visibility means greater power, in a world where people have come to increasingly believe that anything reported on TV is important and anything not reported is insignificant.

This raises an issue that most of us are beginning to discern in the political arena. Suddenly, we are seeing candidates designed to appeal to us instead of leaders who have burning convictions. A persistent complaint relating to the current president is that his positions are based on yesterday's polls. Equally worrisome is the candidate who runs on a constructed image but has a much less acceptable actual agenda.

One example of how far we've come is the case of the 1983 Chicago mayoral race. The mayor, Jane Byrne, was trailing badly in the polls:

> Though eventually losing in a close race, incumbent Jane Byrne managed, through transformation, to achieve a spectacular rise in the polls. Under attack, Byrne hired New York political consultant and former filmmaker David Sawyer to guide her faltering campaign. Sawyer completely changed Byrne's look—hair, dress, make-up, walk—even

managing to alter her abrasive personal demeanor. He
created commercials to support her new image and then
delivered that image to the voters. . . . The new Jane Byrne
was now soft spoken, level headed, responsible—*a blurred
merger of fact and fiction.* (*High Visibility,* emphasis added)

What is amazing about this transformation is that it
took place right in front of the people's eyes. It wasn't as if
she was some unknown who created an image that the
people would want. She was the mayor! The city knew her
well. Yet she underwent a very obvious, self-serving, major
transformation right in the midst of a campaign and
achieved "a spectacular rise in the polls."

KENNEDY WON. NO SWEAT!

Manufactured images are the name of the game in
politics today. The lesson was first learned by Richard
Nixon in 1960. That was when the first televised
presidential debate was held. Nixon treated it as just
another campaign stop. Kennedy took time off to prepare.
Nixon looked tired, moody, and sweaty under the camera
lights. Kennedy looked relaxed and confident. The race
was over that night.

Michael Dukakis was ruined because he looked foolish
when he wore a soldier's helmet and rode around in a tank.
Bob Dole was finished the minute that Jay Leno and David
Letterman decided to make fun of his age every night on
their programs. None of these issues had anything to do with
substantive policy issues, but today, image, not policy, rules.

As Henry Kissinger has said, politicians used to ask him
what to do. Now, they ask him what to say.

IT MUST BE REAL; I SAW IT ON TV!

The lines between reality and fantasy are being blurred
on every level today. For example, did you know that a full

70 percent of the news you read in the newspaper was actually written by press agents and public relations experts who put the spin their clients desire on the report?

But it's not just the representatives of companies and business interests who put a spin on the news. We always get a kick out of the networks around election time devoting so much time to pointing out how the various parties have *spin doctors* who put the spin they want on a particular issue, speech, or campaign promise. Yet as we sit and watch in our homes, it should be obvious (though it is not to many) that the true spin doctors are the media representatives themselves who are telling us how we should see these political spin doctors.

The lines have become so blurred between the real world and the manufactured world that we came to a point in the 1992 U.S. presidential campaign where the vice president of the United States was carrying on a running debate with a completely fictional character called Murphy Brown. It was amazing to watch the power of the fictional world taking control in a situation where the writers could take shot after shot at the vice president on prime-time television and then make fun of him for not recognizing it was just a fictional character he was debating!

But today's audiences, it seems, can't tell the difference anymore anyway. A recent *Times Mirror* poll found that 50 percent of those watching reality shows such as *Cops* or *Rescue 911* believed they were watching the real thing even though a clear statement was on the bottom of the screen saying it was a reenactment.

Or how about this one? Some home owners in Malibu were awarded a $75 million judgment from the California Department of Transportation. The home owners' committee had to choose a judge they could all trust to distribute the money. They chose Judge Wapner of the *People's Court*!

OUR POINT, AND WE DO HAVE ONE!

We live in an extremely complex world. Knowledge in every field is literally exploding. Getting a handle on it all is impossible. How can you develop a coherent worldview when you can't understand 90 percent of what's going on around you?

That's why the media exert such powerful influences upon our culture. The media provide easy answers. Mysteries are solved in ninety minutes. The bad guys are bad and the good guys are good. And *Headline News* can take you around the world in thirty minutes.

Today, our stories, traditions, heroes, and villains all come from the movies and television. But as we've seen, it is a created world, not the real one. And he who defines that world controls our culture. On top of that, it is no longer just the culture of North America being shaped—it is beliefs and values of the entire world.

> *I took a speed-reading course and read* War and Peace *in twenty minutes. It involves Russia.*
>
> *—Woody Allen*

In Chapter 3 we told you about the experience we had the night we were coming home from the Indiana Jones movie, and we saw that light shining from the bottom of the lake. Because we had just seen *Raiders of the Lost Ark*, we thought this light might hold the key to some great and mysterious adventure. Had we just been to see *Jaws*, how likely do you think we would have been to go into that water?

As we discussed, the different reaction would have come about because we would have a different context loaded into our minds. But the bigger point is that a much larger, all-encompassing context is being loaded into our minds on a daily basis by today's culture providers—the mass media.

The media tell us who we are and who they are; who we should be and what we should believe; what we should embrace and what we must detest. The media paint possible futures for the world. The media show some in a rosy light and ridicule others, all solely at the discretion of the painters. And people never even seem to suspect that in the midst of the fabulous entertainment and instant information, they are being transformed from the inside out.

Is this just happening by chance? No way! Even the liberal *New York Times* labels the television networks' cooperative efforts to subtly shape and change public opinion on political, social, and environmental issues as an attempt to achieve "nothing less than a change in American social norms." Industry insider Jay Winstein warns that we have embarked on a road that leads to nothing short of "the application of Madison Avenue expertise to affect the population through mass-media."

Hollywood attorney and environmental activist Bonnie Reiss is so convinced that the mass media can covertly modify public perception that she has left her job to use her influence to have environmental themes weaved into television, movies, and music. "I [feel] that there are a few thousand people who could affect a few million," she claims. And former NBC Chairman Grant Tinker is quite straightforward about the whole thing. "If we can start changing attitudes in this country we can start changing behavior," he says.

ONE WORLD, ONE MIND

And the American media's reach now extends throughout the world. We recently interviewed a man by the name of Richard Gabriel for one of our videos. He is an expert on Middle Eastern and Russian affairs. He pointed out that something unique is happening today. Millions of people from isolated corners of the planet are learning English by watching CNN and American movies! There is no doubt that if they are learning language, they are also learning the cultural values espoused by Hollywood—which they all take to be American values. What we are witnessing is forging of the first global culture in world history, right? Well, not exactly.

LET'S BUILD A TOWER!

In the times of Genesis humankind spoke one language. But that meant more than just sharing common words. People shared a common culture, values, and beliefs. So one day they decided that they would get together and build a tower that would reach into the heavens.

They weren't trying to build a million-mile-high tower. They were building an astrological observatory that would allow them to further develop their common mythology. Most of us know the story:

> And the LORD came down to see the city and the tower, which the children of men builded. And the LORD said, Behold, the people is one, and they have all one language; and this they begin to do: and now nothing will be restrained from them, which they have imagined to do. Go to, let us go down, and there confound their language, that they may not understand one another's speech. . . . Therefore is the name of it called Babel; because the LORD did there confound the language of all the earth: and from thence did the LORD scatter them abroad upon the face of all the earth. (Gen. 11:5–9)

God knew that if all the people did indeed unite as one, in their fallen state, the outcome would be disastrous. After all, the basis of their unity was an astrological tower.

God gave a reason for destroying that tower and scattering the people across the face of the earth. He foresaw that if they were allowed to continue, "nothing will be restrained from them, which they have imagined to do."

Part of this power of unity came from the power of the occult forces that the entire world was tapping into. As we will see in the next chapter, the same powers are being summoned as the uniting force of our world today. However, there was also power in the unity of mind, thought, and belief.

From that day until this, humankind has been divided into different cultures and languages. But today, for the first time in many thousands of years, we are making great progress in countering God's plan with one of our own:

> Take simultaneous language translation. Crude software programs already can take e-mail written in English and translate it to totally unrelated languages like Japanese—albeit with a lot of mistakes. CompuServe, the popular commercial online service with access in 150 countries, has just opened a worldwide forum in which messages can be automatically translated between English, French and German. Over the next 25 years, with computing power roughly doubling every 18 months, it's conceivable that we'll be able to master the very tricky art of reliably translating natural languages in real time. But it's a big debate among those who are working on this problem, and some think it will take longer. Once it's solved, what happens then? Anything you write could be read by anyone on the planet in his or her native tongue. You could pick up the telephone, or its successor the video phone, and hold a real-time conversation with anyone in any country.

BABBLING TOWERS SPRINGING UP EVERYWHERE

However, when we speak of humankind's effort to fight against the Babel effect, we are not speaking primarily about a common language. We are speaking of the first global, united culture since the Tower of Babel. Today, as we travel throughout the world and see television antennas perched on hilltops, and satellite transmitters beside the TV studios, we wonder if these are the modern-day replacements for the Tower of Babel. After all, television is the first progress humankind has made in trying to undo what God did back at the Tower of Babel. Through today's global television programming, a global culture is being restored—just in time for humankind's final bid to build a kingdom without God!

CHAPTER 10

Because of what you have done, the heavens have truly become part of man's world. For one priceless moment in the whole history of man, all of the people on this Earth are truly one.
—*President Richard M. Nixon*
(on the first lunar landing)

AS SEEN ON TV

T hat's one small step for man, one giant leap for mankind."

"Cut! Neil, you've got to say it a little more slowly. Say it like you're really experiencing something out of this world. Let's try it again. Back on the ladder. Okay. Lights. Camera. Action!"

"That's one small step for man, one giant leap for mankind."

"Excellent. That's a wrap. Okay, Buzz, Neil, ditch the suits. We'll tape the moon walk after lunch."

COULD IT HAVE HAPPENED?

All of us who were alive at the time remember where we were on that July day in 1969. And we all remember looking at the moon that night in a way we never had before. After all, it's not every day that someone walks on the moon for the first time.

Yet how do we know it really happened? How do we know that Neil Armstrong and Buzz Aldrin walked on the moon that day? Well, we all answer, we saw it on television!

But wait a minute. We can also see men walking alongside dinosaurs in *Jurassic Park*. We saw Forrest Gump shaking hands with John F. Kennedy in the recent Oscar-winning movie. And we've met Klingons, Romulans, and Cardassians on *Star Trek*.

What's the difference? The answer is that these are movies while the moon landing was a real event. Okay, fair enough. So, tell us, how do you know it was a real event?

If you're not a scientist, deep space radar operator, or a member of the NASA team, the fact is that you know it happened only because you've been told it happened. Clearly, you were not at the Sea of Tranquillity that day. You were not within eyesight of the moon's surface. And the fact is that you could not tell if Neil Armstrong was really on the moon's surface or on a Hollywood sound stage.

We are not suggesting that Neil Armstrong did not walk on the moon. We're just pointing out how much we rely on the mass media to tell us what is happening in our world (and beyond).

HOUSTON, WE'VE GOT A PROBLEM!

But is there a clear line between fiction and reality? Earlier we mentioned the case of Dan Quayle, the vice president of the United States, carrying on a running debate with a fictional character—Murphy Brown. Think about what we know about politics. Today, the images, positions, and sound bites spoken by candidates are carefully crafted by their handlers and media consultants.

Thus, just as the real *brains* behind Murphy Brown's every word were the screenwriters and network bosses, shouldn't we consider that the real *brains* behind Quayle's character were his image makers? So, weren't both characters fictional—at least to some degree?

And there's the rub. The lines between what is real and what is fictional in today's media are becoming increasingly blurred. In such a world, the potential for massive manipulation of the masses is staggering. Consider the following scenario.

DIGITAL DECEPTION: THE WEAPON OF A NEW MILLENNIUM

[AP]Baghdad—Saddam Hussein, the dictatorial leader who withstood the joint forces of the world, was removed from power today. Hussein was overthrown by a popular uprising sparked by footage of him drinking alcohol and eating pork. Both of these activities are at odds with Muslim traditions. Despite withstanding the armies of the world, Hussein could not withstand the pressure from the millions of Muslims who felt betrayed by his actions. In the meantime, it has been learned that the footage of Hussein drinking alcohol and eating pork had actually been digitally created and fed to Iraqi television by the CIA.

Is such a thing possible? Of course, it is. Anyone who has seen the movie *Forrest Gump* has seen how digital technology can now be used to edit a person into a scene where he has never actually been. The creators of the movie were able to edit Gump into a White House ceremony with John F. Kennedy. If you've seen the movie, you saw how seamless it was.

The possibilities are quickly becoming endless. As cinematography expert Victor Burgin says,

One of the nice things you can do with the technology as it's advanced now, on your own desk top, is you can take a videotape or a laserdisk of a film, and you can send the signal to the computer and watch the film on the screen. You can stop it, reverse it, put it in slow-motion and so on. . . . The computer gives you the power to shift everything around in the film. I can take a character from one scene, *store the character in the attitude I've selected, and then I can move that character into any one of the other scenes.* (Emphasis added)

Wow! What Burgin is saying is that he could take, for example, an image of Israeli Prime Minister Benjamin Netanyahu in a certain attitude, say laughing at a joke, and then insert the image of him into a scene where someone was pleading an emotional case and have the prime minister seem to be laughing at him.

These are very real issues that we face in the digital world of today where it will be almost impossible to tell what is real and what is not. Furthermore, in a day when virtually everything we know about the world comes from the media, the potential for outright fraud, in addition to manipulation, is something we should be very aware of. Yet most people never even give it a thought.

GIVE ME A BREAK!

Media expert Michael Medved comments that one of the most ridiculous arguments ever presented is Hollywood's claim that its movies do not affect society. We won't get into the argument here because the truth is so self-evident.

Television: A medium. So called because it is neither rare nor well done.

—Ernie Kovacs

However, let us point out that the American Psychiatric Association studied the issue and concluded that "TV and film violence is responsible for 50 percent of the violence in our society." One of its members, Dr. Brandon Centerwall, estimates that "there would be 10,000 fewer murders, 70,000 fewer rapes, one million fewer motor vehicle thefts, 2.5 million fewer burglaries and ten million fewer larcenies each year [in the U.S.] if not for violent TV and movies."

Media images from the real world have a tremendous effect on society as well. Think of the reaction to the two-minute grainy video that showed police officers beating Rodney King. No one can deny the effect that the video, and subsequent acquittal of the officers, had on an understandably upset black community.

Now, imagine if selected images were purposely fed to the population. Could society not then be molded by those who controlled those images? In a thought-provoking thesis on this issue entitled "Has Reality Become Only Screen Deep?" Gerrit du Preez concludes,

> The media is not an innocent witness to, but rather an active agent in societal changes. The media is not merely bringing the world to our lounges in the form of television, it is fundamentally changing the way things work "out there."

Likewise, media observer Douglas Rushkoff notes that today's media activists "are in command of the most sophisticated techniques of thought control, pattern recognition, and neuro-linguistic programming and use them to create television that changes the way we view reality and thus reality itself."

THE TRIP TO MARS THAT WASN'T

The movie *Capricorn One* came out in 1978. Like our hypothetical moon story at the beginning of the chapter, it tells the story of a staged flight—in this case, to Mars. In this film, the astronauts decide they can no longer go along with the fraud. They then spend the rest of the movie escaping from the "Mars" sound stage and government agents who are trying to kill them before they can tell the world that it was all a fraud.

The director of the film, Peter Hyams, spoke of his motivation in making the film: "So I said, wouldn't it be interesting if you took a major event where the only source that people have is their television screens, and show you how easy it would be to manipulate everybody."

REALITY CAN BE STRANGER THAN FICTION

What does all of this mean? And why is it important? Well, listen to this.

There is widespread recognition that our global information age has made many of the institutions of the past outdated, if not totally useless. The United Nations, for example, is completely ineffectual in dealing with the present global issues. Political alliances, weapons technologies, entire economies, and even our environment are changing so rapidly that many leading voices worry that our entire world system is going to collapse under the weight. That is why we hear such a clear and consistent call for a new world order today. That order would completely restructure everything on the face of the earth to meet the challenges of the new time in which we live.

The million-dollar question, no, make that the billion-dollar question, is this: How do we get from here to there? How can the various cultures and peoples—divided and often at war with each other—be united into one happy global family?

Think of what is required. Peace between Israelites and Arabs and Serbs and Bosnian Muslims. Trust between blacks and whites and French and English. Fair deals between East and West and North and South.

What could possibly unite all of these people? It's difficult to imagine its happening through negotiation no matter how determined the parties involved may be. Think of the Israeli-Arab peace process. Two steps forward, seven steps back. It takes months, or even years, just to get to the table, let alone make progress.

Most students of something called societal evolution look at the situation and say it can't happen without some kind of trigger, some massive, unthinkable event, to push humanity up to the next level. Ervin Laszlo, the former head of the United Nations Institute for Training and Research (UNITAR), sums up the situation this way:

> There's evidence that shows that the present system cannot be indefinitely sustained, that in fact it is already on its last leg. . . . As in nature, so in society, *there is no true evolution without crisis . . . profound and lasting change comes only when the system itself is critically destabilized by new conditions*. . . . Humanity is now approaching a point of critical instability. . . This is the "Checkpoint Charlie" which could mark humanity's passage into a new age—or into oblivion! (Emphasis added)

According to Laszlo, the transformation to a new world order cannot come slowly through negotiation. It will come about only when humankind faces some monumental event that will cause the world to reconsider the way it sees everything. But Laszlo also points out something that should bring our entire discussion into focus:

> Conscious human beings, equipped with a basic knowledge of societal evolution, could exploit whatever degrees of freedom such evolution offers and influence the direction of evolution to their own advantage.
> —Message to Worldview 84 in Washington D.C.

Likewise, the Communications Era Task Force has concluded that because of "our ability to see the historical turning point at which we stand we can more deliberately and consciously influence our direction."

Do you hear what these people are saying? They are suggesting that we need a major crisis to push us into the next level of civilization—a new world order. However, they are also indicating that the process could be controlled or that a fake crisis could be orchestrated to get the world to accept the idea of a new world order.

So, what massive event could possibly change the world community so drastically that it would suddenly forget about the things that divide it and boldly embrace a new order of the ages?

APOCALYPSE NOW

Imagine, so the reasoning goes, that the world turns on the evening news one night and hears that the military arsenal of the former Soviet Union has been seized by rebel forces that have launched a full-scale nuclear attack on the United States. The next announcement is that the U.S. has launched a counterstrike. Suddenly, the world as a whole realizes that the events are completely out of its hands. It is only a matter of moments until most of the world is destroyed.

The father sits with his son, unable to protect him in any way. The mother, in desperation, wants everyone to go to the basement to prolong the certain fate an instant longer, hoping against hope that it is all just a bad dream. Quickly, a sense of common fate sweeps the world. The man in Moscow realizes that the man in Washington is in exactly the same boat. The thousands of miles that once separated their worlds have vanished. The crisis and a common bond through television instantly knit them together in a common hopeless despair.

Now imagine that somehow the crisis is averted. A world leader arises and addresses a world that gives him its full, united attention. He announces how the disaster has been averted and then explains how such an atrocity can never be allowed to take place again. He urges the world audience to realize the oneness of the planet and how they will live or die together. His tirade focuses on petty national, cultural, and religious differences, and he encourages the world to come together as one in this great "spaceship earth."

Such a scenario is not completely unrealistic. Narrowly missing such a disaster, the world could well be ready to accept the compromises and sacrifices a global village would require. Some argue that the change of thinking caused by such a crisis would make the system not only seem desirable but also imperative for the salvation of humankind. Furthermore, such a near disaster could easily cause a worldwide economic collapse, only compounding the need for global systems of recovery. National political alliances would be shattered and totally obsolete in the face of building a world system of governance. Add to this the common problems of environment and population, and the pull toward a global system could be virtually irresistible.

BUT IS IT ENOUGH?

However, many students of societal evolution claim that a crisis such as this would not be enough to push humankind forward into the new age. The problem, they say, is that although a threat to the well-being of the world would show how dangerous the current system is, it would give the world no hope for the future.

Willis Harmen, a former consultant to the National Goals Research Staff of the White House, argues that only a new vision of humankind and its place in the universe can possibly lay the foundation for a new and better world.

SPACE: THE FINAL FRONTIER

One thing that could change the way the world thinks almost overnight would be a close encounter of some type. UFO's have been the subject of much scorn over the last several decades, but it now appears that the technology that made the space shuttle possible, combined with the popularity of movies such as *Star Wars* and now *Independence Day*, has left many millions of people open to the possibility of an extraterrestrial (E.T.) visiting planet earth.

Hal Lindsey, writing his book *The 1980s, Countdown to Armageddon*, laid out just such a scenario:

> Authorities now admit that there have been confirmed sightings of unidentified flying objects. . . . Reports held in U.S. Air Force files reveal that whatever these flying objects are, they move and turn at speeds unmatched by human technology. It is my opinion that UFO's are real and that there will be a proven close encounter of the third kind soon. And I believe that the source of this phenomenon is some type of alien being of great intelligence and power. According to the Bible, a demon is a spiritual personality in a state of war with God. Prophecy tells us that demons will be allowed to use their powers of deception in a grand way during the last days of history. I believe these demons will stage a spacecraft landing on Earth. They will claim to be from an advanced culture in another galaxy. They may even claim to have planted human life on this planet and tell us they have returned to check on our progress. Many scientists, not to mention movies and television shows, are putting forth similar theories about the origin of life on Earth. If demons led by Satan, their chief, did pull off such a deception, then they could certainly lead the world into total error regarding God and His revelation.

WELCOME TO THE TWILIGHT ZONE

Although this is only one example of the type of spiritual event that could transform the world, it shows how much more powerful this type of event would be in changing the world's thinking than a purely natural disaster. An episode of the *New Twilight Zone* laid out a scenario in which during a heated and completely stalled arms reduction session at the U.N., a UFO appeared and hovered over the United Nations complex, then an alien being materialized before all of the delegates.

He explained that he had planted life on this planet and that he had come back to check on their progress. After performing several signs and wonders to convince the nations of his incredible godlike powers, he gave them just twenty-four hours to solve their differences. And they did. The show concluded with this statement: "For those of you who doubt that world peace is possible, remember that it happened first in the twilight zone."

Almost as if he had seen that particular episode, Ronald Reagan shared the same idea when he first met Mikhail Gorbachev in 1985. As they sought to find an end to the cold war, he reflected on how a close encounter would cut through all the preliminaries and instantaneously unite the world:

> If suddenly there was a threat to this world from some other species from another planet, we'd forget all the little local differences that we have between our two countries, and we would find out once and for all that we really are all human beings on this earth together.

Now, as you know, we've talked about this very concept several times in this book. That is because we believe that the subject of E.T.'s and other worlds will be very much at the heart of the Antichrist's rise to power.

Imagine that a UFO did land in New York City. It would change the world's belief system overnight. Think about it. It would instantly change our view of the universe and our place in it. It would, without a doubt, pose the greatest challenge to the Christian worldview that could be imagined.

And let's not forget that in today's world, where the lines between reality and deception have been virtually erased, such an encounter could even be staged. For the purposes of manipulation, it doesn't matter if UFO's are real or not. It only matters that people believe they are real!

GOD WILL PROVIDE THE TRIGGER!

The fact is that we know what event is going to trigger the transformation into a new world order. It is the rapture of the church, and the Bible laid out the scenario for us thousands of years ago.

We've already explained that the rapture is that moment in time when every true believer in Jesus Christ will suddenly vanish off the face of the earth. Boy, if you want a transformational event that is going to blow the mind of the world, that is it. The rapture is going to literally trigger the complete change of thinking on the whole planet. These other events may well serve as smoke screens or as secondary events related to the coming transformation. But the rapture is the event that is going to change everything.

And this is where we believe that UFO's will come into play. Think about it for a second. What is the only context that this world has for people vanishing from right before their eyes? It is *Star Trek*'s transporter beam. You know—"Beam me up, Scotty." That is why we believe that people won't feel as if they've been left behind. Instead, they will thank their lucky stars that they've been spared.

The more we've thought about it, the more this idea of UFO's seems to fit with Satan's lie and his plan to deceive humankind during the Tribulation period. After all, it provides a convenient explanation for where those who vanished have gone. The idea that other races and species from various planets exist would give human beings the idea that they can become even more highly evolved than they are. And that gets to the core of the deception that lies ahead.

THE GARDEN OF EDEN: TAKE 2

Earlier we mentioned Willis Harman, a former consultant to the National Goals Research Staff of the White House. When speaking of the search for a potential bond that could unite the world, he concluded there is only one idea that could prove strong enough to capture the hearts and minds of people. He pointed to the startling discoveries in the area of psychic powers, ESP, parapsychology, telekinesis, and telepathic communications and said that only the global acceptance of these new powers can bring humankind together:

> If such a paradigm, involving a basic shift in the accepted vision of reality, were to become the basis of presently industrialized society, its institutionalization would amount to one of the most thoroughgoing transformations in the history of mankind. We might apply to such a change the Greek word *metanoia*: a fundamental shift in mind, as in a religious conversion.

It's remarkable that this idea of expanded human powers is being offered as the single belief system that can unite the world into a common belief. This is likely the exact story that the Antichrist will foist upon the world when he arrives on the scene. And the idea of a world joined together by occult beliefs goes right back to the Tower of Babel—humankind's last attempt to construct a global village.

YOU HAVE PSYCHIC POWERS?
TELL IT TO THE NICE DOCTOR!

While it seems a little far-fetched that the world would embrace this New Age mumbo jumbo today, consider how much more the world will open to such exotic ideas after millions of people have vanished off the face of the earth.

Suddenly, the old rules don't apply any more. Clearly, something will have happened that does not fit with today's ideas of science and reason. In addition to that, the apostle Paul warned that the Antichrist will arrive on the scene showing "all power and signs and lying wonders" (2 Thess. 2:9).

Moreover, he won't be the only one. Jesus Himself warned us that there would be many "false Christs, and false prophets," showing "great signs and wonders" who would be so powerful that, if God allowed it, they would deceive even the strongest believers (Matt. 24:24).

SHIRLEY, YOU JEST

You see, the power of the Antichrist's lie will be not only his claim that he is a god, but also his claim that anyone who wants can become one too. All people have to do is tap into their own internal powers. As actress and New Age guru Shirley MacLaine sums it up:

> You are everything. Everything you want to know is inside of you. You are the Universe. . . . Maybe the tragedy of the human race was that we had forgotten that we were each divine. . . . You must never worship anyone or anything other than self. For you are God. To love self is to love God. . . . I know that I exist, therefore I am. I know that the God source exists, therefore it is. Since I am part of that force, then I AM that I AM.
>
> —*Out on a Limb*, Bantam Books, 1983

Wow! You can't get more to the point than that. And no wonder, if people are performing miracles all over the place, that people will believe they indeed can become as gods, just as the Antichrist tells them they can. Unfortunately for those deceived souls, it is the same lie that caused Adam and Eve to eat the forbidden fruit in the Garden of Eden—"Ye shall be as gods" (Gen. 3:5).

THE HIDDEN AGENDA

What is amazing to watch today is how the plans of human beings, Satan, and God are all converging at the exact same point in time. Humankind knows that its systems are not working. Despite the advances in science and humanism, wars and hatred rule the globe.

Sometimes well-intentioned, and sometimes selfish, globalists are looking for a way to propel humankind into a new order that they can control. Whether it is achieved by deceit or fraud is not important. They never recognize the unseen spiritual hand in the background using their plans and efforts to bring forth his kingdom—the kingdom of the Antichrist. Yet, somehow, that angel of deception cannot see how all of this is unfolding exactly as God said it would.

Go!

_____
_____
_____
_____
_____
_____
_____
_____
_____
_____
_____
_____
_____
_____
_____
_____
_____

CRUISING THE SUPERHIGHWAY

CYBERSPACE WEDDING

Do I look all right? Is my hair okay? How about my dress? My dress is too tight, isn't it? I look like a sausage, for crying out loud. Who wants to marry a sausage?"

"Relax, Susie, you've just got the wedding day jitters. Trust me. I'm your mother. Would your own mother lie to you? You look fabulous, and your dress is perfect. Frank's going to take one look at you, and he'll know right away that he's the luckiest man on earth."

"Do you really think so, Mom?"

"Of course I do, dear. Now what else can I help you with?"

"You could help me find the right corsage for the bridesmaids."

"Of course, dear, let me have a look at the fabric so I can make sure I get a perfect match."

Susie grabs a piece of fabric and holds it up to the little camera mounted on the computer monitor in front of her. She is relieved to see her mother's approving smile on the screen.

"That looks fantastic, dear, just give me a few minutes and I'll look after the corsages for you." She chooses "save image" and goes right to work.

Mom clicks on the menu at the top of her computer screen and starts browsing through the on-line shopping mall. Fish, flags, flooring, florists. "Here we go." She clicks on a little picture of a rose bouquet and types in Irvine, California. Instantly, a list of all the florists in the Irvine area pops up in front of her. She chooses one, and a friendly face appears on her screen. "Welcome to Jennifer's Flowers. How can I help you today?"

"I need six bridesmaids' corsages to match this fabric." She clicks on the picture captured from Susie moments before.

"Oh, that's beautiful," says the friendly face at the flower shop. The clerk shows Susie's mom several pictures of corsages and she picks one. Seconds later, Susie is looking at the final selection on her screen.

"The corsages will all be delivered before 11:00 A.M., so the girls will get them in lots of time."

"Thanks, Mom. They're perfect for a sunny spring day like this one."

Susie's mom nods and smiles. "At least you have sunshine out there in California. It's raining and miserable here in Maine," she says.

"I wonder what the weather is like in Singapore right now?" Susie muses. "Could you click over to Frank and ask him? You know I'm not supposed to see him before the wedding."

Does this sound like something out of a futuristic movie? Or at least a futuristic soap opera? Well, hang on to your hats, the future is now! On Valentine's Day 1996 a California couple tied the knot in a tiny chapel in a town called Worlds Away. But what made the wedding so unusual was that the chapel, and the town, don't really exist. At least not here in the real world. The wedding was hosted by CompuServe, the giant on-line computer service, and the bride, groom, minister, and guests were all in different parts of the country. Welcome to cyberspace!

WHAT IS CYBERSPACE?

When William Gibson was writing his chilling futuristic novel *Neuromancer* way back in 1984, he spent a lot of time observing young people playing computer games in the local arcade.

He noticed that their bodies and minds were completely absorbed, as though they had actually entered the world projected on the screen in front of them. Kids playing the games developed a "belief that there's some kind of space behind the screen. Some place that you can't see, but you know is there." He called that place cyberspace, and today, that same term is used to describe *the world inside the computer.*

> For a list of all the ways technology has failed to improve the quality of life, please press 3.
> —*Alice Kahn*

Chances are, unless you've been living in a cave, you've heard about cyberspace too, although you may have heard it called by one of its other names, such as the Net, the electronic frontier, or the information superhighway. If you adopt the definition chosen by computer activist John Barlow, you may even have been there without knowing it. You see, Barlow defines cyberspace as "that place you are when you're talking on the telephone." But whatever we call it, or however we define it, the phenomenon is a real one, and it's destined to change this generation in ways that we can't even begin to imagine.

THE NET

If the story of the 1980s has been the phenomenal evolution of the computer, then the story of the 1990s would have to be the Internet. Growing at speeds faster than industry insiders can even begin to keep track of, some estimates are that the Internet's core, the World Wide Web, grew by a staggering 350,000 percent in 1994 alone!

No technology in the history of the world has ever grown so quickly, not the telephone, not the fax machine, not even the personal computer. (This is especially shocking when we consider that American families bought more computers than television sets in 1995.) Conservative estimates put the population of cyberspace at close to a billion by the year 2000. And estimates have to be conservative, because if the current growth rates were to continue, then the population of cyberspace would *exceed the population of the world* by 2003.

WELCOME TO THE WORLD WIDE WEB

Today, when you hear people talking about the Internet, they are almost always talking about something called the World Wide Web. The World Wide Web is like a giant interactive television network with literally millions of channels called home pages or Web sites. Anyone who has an account with a local Internet service provider can have a home page, and not surprisingly, most people do. And the result has been an absolute avalanche of information, some of it even useful, at our fingertips.

There are home pages built around every topic under the sun, and chances are, no matter what you may be interested in, you can find someone who shares your interest, somewhere on the Web. There are home pages for people who love cats, for people who hate cats, even for people who hate people who love cats. There is even a home page with a continuously updated picture of some guy's fish tank. That's it. That's all it does. And yet thousands of people each day check in to have a look at the "fish-cam." You see, in this cyberworld, your home page can stand right there beside IBM, McDonald's, and the United States government, competing for visitors in the vast world of cyberspace.

And talk about growth! The most recent statistics show a new home page coming on-line every four seconds. The total number of Web sites now doubles every fifty days.

But How Do You Find Anything in the Digital Jungle?

With all of this information coming on-line, how can we ever hope to find what we're looking for? Fortunately, a variety of "search engines" allow you, believe it or not, to search through millions and millions of pages of information to find exactly what you're looking for. How many pigs in Poland? How much does the earth weigh? Who's the guest on David Letterman next Tuesday? The Internet can find you answers to almost anything, all in less than a few seconds.

One of the most popular search engines is Digital Corporation's AltaVista Search, and this statement on the home page says it all: *AltaVista gives you access to the largest Web index: 30 million pages found on 275,600 servers, and four million articles from 14,000 UseNet news groups. It is accessed over 21 million times per weekday.* There's no doubt about it. We are living in the information age.

The World at Your Fingertips

Just to give you an idea of how much stuff is out there, we tried entering a few subjects into AltaVista to see what it might find. Here are the number of "hits" registered for various topics:

SUBJECT	NO. OF HOME PAGES
Bible Prophecy	500
Caribou Hunting	87
Dog Food	3,000
Earthquakes	9,000
Tonya Harding	1,000
President Warren Harding	143
The Internet	10,292,747
Christian	300,000

By the way, one of the hits on the Bible Prophecy search is our very own *This Week in Bible Prophecy* home page. If you're interested, and have access to the Internet, our address is www.twibp.com. Oh, yes, and one other interesting note. If you're wondering how comprehensive these searches are, consider this. While searching for a listing of the most popular Web sites, we managed to misspell the word *popular*, typing instead *popluar*. AltaVista found 205 hits on the word *popluar*, all of which were typos like ours.

WHAT IS FUELING ALL THIS GROWTH?

Now that you have some appreciation of how quickly the information superhighway is growing, let's take a minute to review some of the reasons underlying its incredible success.

First, a little history. The Internet was originally conceived and designed by a man named Larry Roberts in the early 1960s. It wasn't called the Internet then. It was called ARPAnet, and it was born purely as a result of the cold war. Commissioned by the military, the U.S. government was attempting to create a communication system that could survive a massive nuclear attack. The idea was to deliver messages in "packets" that could travel along any number of different paths to their destination. If an entire city was wiped out, the messages would simply take a different route, and so the Internet was born.

Today, the Internet has been built upon that original foundation, and because it merely "piggybacks" on the existing telephone system, its rapid growth has been relatively easy to accomplish. You see, there were no trenches to dig, no cables to bury, no telephone poles to erect across the country. By using the wires and cables that were already in place, the Internet was able to cover most of the civilized world almost overnight.

> The most overlooked advantage to owning a computer is that if they foul up there's no law against whacking them around a little.
>
> —Porterfield

And as we talk about all of the advantages that have helped the Internet grow the way it has, let's not forget the most important thing of all— it's a great product! Clearly, the Internet represents some pretty remarkable technology, and thanks to the multimedia capabilities of the World Wide Web, people simply can't wait to get hooked up. A recent *Time*/CNN poll showed that while 57 percent of Americans didn't know what cyberspace was, 85 percent were sure that it had made their lives better! Besides, to a generation of TV junkies the move to the World Wide Web didn't seem like a very big step at all. Many considered it to be the natural evolution of media. For most, the transition from couch potato to mouse potato was a seamless one.

Perhaps the most important factor in the rapid expansion of the Net has been the price. For most people, this technology is quite affordable when you consider what you're getting for your money. You can make phone calls over the Net, do your shopping, pay your bills, write letters, and research just about anything. You can even watch TV and listen to the radio right there at your personal computer. Sure, the hardware is a little more expensive than a good TV, but the price is coming down all the time, and it won't be long until a computer with access to the Internet will be as indispensable as a TV or a telephone is today.

HOW CLOSE ARE WE?

To take the step into the virtual world of cyberspace via the Internet, you need two things: a computer with a modem and a telephone line. That's it. So right away, almost everyone in North America is halfway there, when you consider that more than 98 percent of American homes have telephones. As for the computers, the figure is getting very close to 50 percent and that number is increasing with lightning-like speed. And the number of computer-equipped homes is going to expand even more rapidly in the next few years thanks to increasing power and plummeting prices.

> *Programming today is a race between software engineers striving to build bigger and better idiot-proof programs, and the Universe trying to produce bigger and better idiots. So far, the Universe is winning.*
> —*Rich Cook*

Several major companies are working on terminals that will allow full access to the Internet for less than the price of a new TV. So can Americans afford that price? Only 2 percent of American homes don't have a color TV. Why? Because it has become a necessity in today's world. Enough said.

GLOBAL COMMUNICATIONS NETWORK

So far, we've been talking about North America, but the Internet's real power is that it is going to be a totally global phenomenon. Up until now, there has been a big problem with this dream of a united on-line world. While telephones are a fixture in virtually every home in the United States, more than half the world's population lives more than two hours from the nearest telephone. It is very expensive to string telephone line, and without significant economic potential, no company is willing to foot the bill to run phone lines into the remote parts of the world.

Today, however, with advances in satellite and cellular phone technologies, the possibility of a world completely connected electronically is no longer just a dream. The giant electronics corporation, Motorola, is working on a project that plans by 1998 to have the whole world within range of a telecommunications satellite. The corporation plans to do this by surrounding the earth in an array of satellites, a monumental, but realistic task. In the world of wireless communication, a world that is literally just around the corner, you really can reach out and touch someone, no matter where he or she is.

Another major player in this ambitious project to bring the world together electronically is none other than Microsoft founder and chairman, Bill Gates. Together with Craig McCaw of McCaw Cellular, Gates has formed the Teledesic Corporation, which plans to add a fleet of more than eight hundred satellites to those already orbiting the earth. To give you some idea of just how many satellites they're talking about, consider that this project would more than double the number of satellites now in orbit! Their goal is simply "to bring the information super-highway in all its glory to even the most remote reaches of the globe by the end of the century."

With so many satellites in orbit around the earth, no matter where you are, you would be assured of always having at least one passing overhead. As well as making sure that everyone would be in contact, this satellite blanket would mean that much, much less powerful earth-based stations would be needed to use the technology.

According to insiders, "all you would need is a battery-powered station and an 18-inch antenna. That would allow even the poorest countries to get connected."

YOU AIN'T SEEN NOTHING YET!

So here we see the groundwork being laid for a world united as few dreamed possible just a few short years ago. Keep in mind though, as impressive as all this may be, you ain't seen nothing yet.

And this isn't just another one of those pipe dreams, such as flying from New York to Paris in twenty minutes or flying the cars like George Jetson has in the Saturday morning cartoons. While these feats may be possible someday, they are certainly not imminent. When it comes to a world united electronically through the information superhighway, however, we're not waiting for any technological breakthroughs to make it all possible. The technology to hurl us into the future *is already here*. We're waiting for it to be *put into place*!

The cyberspace that we spend our time in five years from now will make today's technology look like something from the Dark Ages. By that time people will look back on the state of the world today and wonder how we ever managed to survive without the technology that they take for granted.

WE NEED A BIGGER PIPE

What are we waiting for? For the most part the answer is one thing—bandwidth. In the simplest terms, bandwidth refers to the amount of information that can be squeezed through the information pipeline. Think about the Internet for a moment. Bandwidth is the only thing standing in the way of being able to offer such incredible value through the Net that TV itself might become a thing of the past. You could, for example, visit our *This Week in Bible Prophecy* home page and select any of our past episodes to watch, right there on your computer. The technology to make this possible already exists, but to do it properly, we would have to be able to find a way to send more information through the Internet pipeline.

To clarify the bandwidth issue, imagine, if you will, trying to fill up a backyard swimming pool using a garden hose. If you own a pool, chances are, you don't have to imagine it. It takes days! Now, imagine filling it up with a fire hose. You could fill the whole thing in a couple of hours. Finally, imagine a six-foot-wide concrete conduit pouring water into your pool, filling it in a matter of minutes.

Going back to the Internet, the vast majority of today's Internet connections are made through the copper phone wires, antiques of a generation gone by. These are the garden hoses of the information age. Some cities are now hooking up Internet users through the coaxial cable systems that bring us cable TV. That coaxial cable is the fire hose. But increasingly, the world is being connected with something called fiber optics, tiny threads of glass capable of carrying mind-boggling amounts of information through cyberspace. As you have probably guessed, fiber optics are the concrete conduits in the information age.

THROUGH THE LOOKING GLASS

In terms of actual information, here is what the differences in bandwidth can mean. A copper telephone wire can carry about ten thousand bits per second, slightly less than all the text contained in one page of this book. A coaxial cable can carry ten million bits per second, the equivalent of about one five-hundred-page novel. A fiber - optic cable can carry ten billion bits per second, or about one hundred of those five-hundred-page novels! The increases are literally staggering as we move into these faster transmission methods, and the capabilities that they will bring to the information superhighway will be almost beyond belief. And yet rest assured, within a few short years, people will find themselves needing even more.

Again, before we move on to look at the future of cyberspace, remember, this technology already exists. It's just a matter of getting the cables laid down and the world wired up.

Imagine it, in the world of medicine, specialists will be able to examine patients a thousand miles away. Teachers will be able to teach a virtual classroom of students made up of kids living in twelve countries. Every student of physics will be able to "sit in" on lectures by Stephen Hawking. Busy parents will do all of their grocery shopping without leaving the house.

CYBERSHOPPING

Obviously, a big part of any system like this one is going to be commercial, so shopping in cyberspace is going to become a reality in the very near future.

Already, sales on the Internet are nearing the $1 billion mark annually, but that number is expected to swell to nearly $20 billion by the end of the century. The day is probably not far off when the vast majority of our shopping is done in cyberspace, and not long after that people will wonder how we ever managed to live without it.

"Ah, come on, Grandpa, you've got to be kidding. You expect us to believe that when you wanted a new jacket, you had to actually go out to a big building full of clothes and look for one you liked?" A statement like this may seem a long way off, but don't laugh. It's closer than you think.

HOW MUCH FOR JERRY SEINFELD'S JACKET?

Bill Gates, founder and chairman of Microsoft, the world's leading computer software company, envisions a day when television and the Internet will be so interwoven that you'll literally be able to combine entertainment and shopping. Let's say you're lying on the couch, watching a rerun of *Seinfeld* on TV.

You notice that the star of the show is wearing a jacket that you really like, so you reach for your remote. You point it at the TV, and a small red dot appears on the screen. You move it over to Jerry's jacket and click the little blue button on the clicker in your hand. On screen, a little white window pops up and tells you that the jacket is genuine leather, comes in three sizes, and costs $119. You click on "large" and "okay" and that's it. The very next day, a jacket just like Jerry's is delivered to your door. You don't even have to worry about paying for it, since the money was automatically deducted from your account the instant you clicked "okay."

GOOD-BYE, RETAIL; HELLO, QVC

Don't laugh at those goofy TV shopping shows that seem to run twenty-four hours a day on some stations. They are giving you a glimpse of the future, and someday soon, we'll all be doing our shopping that way.

And what about the millions of retail stores that line our streets and fill our shopping malls? They will become things of the past in the world of interactive computing. Many of you are thinking, *What, you think I'll be too lazy to go downtown to buy a pair of sandals?* Absolutely not, although for many of us that is a distinct possibility. You can probably imagine people a dozen years ago looking at these new remote control TV clickers and saying, "It'll be a sad day when I'm too lazy to walk over to the TV to change channels." Try to find someone today who prefers changing channels the *old-fashioned* way.

Still, in the case of cybershopping, it's not that we'll be too lazy to go shopping; retail stores won't be able to compete.

Think about the expenses of opening and operating a shoe store at the local mall. You need to pay for rent, utilities, staff, inventory, insurance, blah, blah, blah. That makes it very difficult to compete with the guy whose only real expense is the shoes. That's why television shopping programs have become such an incredible phenomenon in the present day. Giant networks like QVC can mark up their products 100 percent and still sell stuff for a whole lot less than their retail competitors whose expenses are so high.

Electronic shopping then will become a reality as people continue to demand low price and convenience. And clearly, when it comes to low price and convenience, it will be hard to compete with cybershopping.

Initially, there is bound to be some resistance to the idea of cybershopping. After all, we've been doing it the old-fashioned way for a long, long time. But consider for a moment the now familiar ATM machine attached to the side of almost every bank in town. At first, people were a little leery of doing business with a machine, but by most estimates, within four years, more than 90 percent of all transactions will be done through either ATM machines or on-line banking. It may take a couple of years for us to adapt, but where convenience and economy are concerned, we always seem to come around.

RACING TOWARD THE MARK OF THE BEAST

It's hard for us to go anywhere these days without people asking us about one of the most famous prophecies of all, the prophecy of the mark of the Beast. After all, the Bible makes it very clear that in the last days, there will be a system in place that allows the Antichrist to track the buying and selling of the entire world. For a detailed examination of this prophecy and how it is being fulfilled, please refer to our book *Racing Toward the Mark of the Beast*. You should be able to find it at any Christian bookstore.

First, let's take a look at the famous prophecy from the book of Revelation:

> And he causeth all, both small and great, rich and poor, free and bond, to receive a mark in their right hand, or in their foreheads: And that no man might buy or sell, save he that had the mark, or the name of the beast, or the number of his name. (Rev. 13:16–17)

After reading as far as you have in this book, and especially in this chapter, the whole idea of someone being able to monitor our buying and selling can't seem very far-fetched. Whatever your beliefs may be about Bible prophecy, you'll still have to admit that the prophecy quoted here is a chilling one indeed.

With the increasing move toward cashlessness in our society, and with electronic banking already here, the addition of electronic shopping, worldwide connectivity, and global interdependence sure make the prophecy of the mark of the Beast seem a lot more realistic than it would have even ten years ago. By the turn of the century it will seem almost inevitable.

UNDOING THE BABEL EFFECT

All this talk about a world united in cyberspace leaves open one very important question. If a stockbroker in New York is linked up electronically to a potential buyer in Stockholm, how in the world are they going to communicate? After all, this is not *Star Trek*. Everyone in the universe doesn't speak perfect English.

Rest assured, as we discussed earlier, there is a solution to this problem. Or at least there will be one soon. A company in Fairfax, Virginia, Globalink, recently introduced a remarkable new piece of software called Web Translator. So far, it is capable of translating any Web page to and from Spanish, English, French, and German in less than twenty seconds!

That's a staggering accomplishment, and you can bet that a lot of work is being done to perfect this technology and to add many more languages to the mix. As computers continue to get faster (remember that computer power *doubles* every eighteen months) and the market continues to demand more, this technology is expected to spread like wildfire, knocking down one of the most substantial barriers to a united world—the barrier of language.

WHAT IF I DON'T WANT TO GO ON-LINE?

"So does all this mean that I'll be forced to go on-line in order to survive in the future?" you ask. We've been asked this question so many times, it would make your head spin. But the answer is simple: Yes and no. First of all, let's make one significant clarification, and that involves the word *forced*. You can be "forced" to do something without having to be threatened with death for not doing it.

Consider the telephone. No one is forced to have a telephone, and quite frankly if you would prefer to live in a shack in the middle of the bush like the Unabomber, you can probably get by without one. But for the most part, life would be terribly inconvenient, and you would be at a fantastic disadvantage if you didn't have one. For most of us, having a phone is a necessity, and thus, life in the world today more or less forces us to have one.

Another example is the credit card. Although many people don't have one, the majority of us do, and most of us have more than one. Why? Because there are a lot of things you can't do without one. One of them is buying stuff from direct response TV commercials. How many times have you heard the expression "Sorry, no COD's"? Feeding that through the universal translator, it comes out as "you better have a credit card." Certainly when most, and eventually all, of our shopping is done in cyberspace, a credit card, or whatever electronic system takes its place, will be a necessity. Maybe we won't be forced to have one. Maybe we'll prefer not to eat.

Like the telephone and the television and the automobile, the Internet is destined to become one of those things that you can't be without. And that fact alone has been proven to be sufficient to put it in every home in the nation.

*Since we're coming to the end of not only a century
but a millennium, no doubt even more demons and
phantoms are about to flood the portals.*
                    —*Hillel Schwartz* (Century's End)

CHAPTER 12

2000 A.D.:
ARE YOU READY?

I agree with you, Jack, this is a world of unbelievable
change. I mean, just think about all the stuff we've been
talking about. There's no question that this generation is
so totally different from any previous generation that it's
just . . . well, it's mind-boggling."

"Let me ask you something, Tom. What do you think
the most powerful development of this generation has
been?"

"That's easy. Technology. You know, computers,
cyberspace, the Internet, virtual reality. How about you?"

"I'd have to say it's the media. No generation before
this one had the unbelievable power of tell-a-vision at
their disposal. The way we can spread ideas and give
people a common vision of the future. That is what's going
to transform this world more than anything else."

"How about you, Tim? You're just sitting there smiling.
What do you think the biggest influence in this generation
will be?"

"What doesn't yet exist, but will exist, that will amplify
the power of everything you've mentioned, and make them
all stronger, without actually doing anything?"

"What is this, *Jeopardy*? You can't answer a question with a question."

"Okay, smart guy. We give up. What isn't, but will be, that is already affecting the entire world?"

"The year 2000."

COMPOUND INTEREST

By now, everyone is beginning to realize that the year 2000 is much more than just another year on the calendar. It is also a symbol and a metaphor. It represents nothing less than our doorway to the future. And it serves as a milestone and a turning point for so many values and belief systems that you can't even begin to count them.

> Many new agers see the turn of the millennium as the beginning of the Age of Aquarius. Futurists see it as the beginning of the global age. UFO cultists see it as the year of contact. And, many Christians also believe that it will be the year in which Jesus returns to earth!

The approach of the year 2000 is actually amplifying every trend in our world today. It is one of, if not *the,* major contributor to the sense of expectancy and anticipation that is sweeping our world today. But it's not only affecting general trends. The year 2000 has the power to completely change the meaning of specific events as well. For example, we've talked about the effect a UFO landing would have on this world. But now imagine its happening on December 31, 1999! Suddenly, it would be a powerful sign that we are entering a new age.

In our prophetic time, when we know deception is at the heart of Satan's plan to win the allegiance of this earth, it is not hard to see how the world can be badly deceived by a well-timed display of his "power signs and lying wonders." As the apostle Paul warned, Satan will come to this world appearing to be nothing less than "an angel of light" (2 Cor. 11:14).

MILLENNIAL FEVER

Before we talk further about the historic moment in which we live, we want to point out that this has all happened before. Do you think the world took the year 1000 in stride? Absolutely not.

Even the turn of a *century* is enough to create a wave of panic. H. G. Wells's infamous novel, *War of the Worlds*, sparked its share of panic not because it spoke of a Martian invasion, but because it was published during the centennial fervor of 1898. Indeed, it was only one of about fifty novels that came out at that time dealing with a Martian invasion. And people believed such a thing was possible because Italian astronomer Giovanni Schiaparelli had discovered that channels scored and crisscrossed the surface of the red planet. The suggestion of intelligent life, combined with the turn of the century, created a potent cocktail that had much of the world ready for anything. Isn't it interesting that Martian life is on the front pages again as this millennium is drawing to a close?

There is no doubt that millennial or centennial madness has been a major phenomenon in the past. There is also no doubt that it is having a major influence in our world today. You just can't deny it. And many people see the Christian view that Jesus is coming soon as nothing more than another symptom of this understandable but dangerous reality. All of this stuff about prophecy, they say, will go away once we can get past the turn of the millennium. Unfortunately, as we shall see, if the Lord does tarry, they may just be right!

TWO VISIONS ON A COLLISION COURSE

The year 2000 is, as we've said, much more than just another year on the calendar. *Time* magazine says that the millennium is really a "cosmic moment" that is packed with

> immense historical symbolism and psychological power. It does not depend on objective calculation, but entirely on what people bring to it—their hopes, their anxieties, the metaphysical focus of their attention. The millennium is essentially an event of the imagination. (Fall 1992)

Throughout history, transitional years, whether they be the turn of the century or the one millennium we've already experienced (in the year 1000), have led most people to think of judgment and the end of the world.

That same tendency holds true for this time in history. However, this time there is a powerful *competing* vision. It is a vision of breakthrough and awakening. It is a vision that sees humankind bursting through a barrier the way cars burst through plastic sheets in those old gasoline commercials.

To be sure, part of it comes from New Age thinking. But more, as *Time* magazine says, comes from our imaginations. Imaginations that have been fueled by Hollywood and the Space Center in Houston, and by our newfound confidence instilled by our incredible technological achievements.

EVIL EMPIRE—NOT

But there is another ingredient in this vision's recipe. It is the world's collective desire to step back from the brink, both physically and emotionally. Let's not forget that not too many years ago we were locked in a cold war. The Soviet Union was the "evil empire." Star Wars missile defense systems were needed to protect against nuclear annihilation. Everyone just wondered how (and when) it would start.

Then the situation changed. Suddenly, almost in a heartbeat, the Soviet Union was no more. Disarmament plans filled the newscasts. The world breathed a sigh of relief. And despite legitimate concerns that the world was celebrating mere rhetoric about disarmament instead of the actual elimination of weapons, a mood of peace swept the world, and the West in particular.

Somehow, about ten years before the turn of the millennium, humankind decided to look forward to the promise of a peaceful world instead of getting stuck in the unfriendly politics of the past.

In with the New, Out with the Old

So, at a moment in history when everything is being amplified by the approaching millennium, and the foundations of the entire planet are being rapidly transformed as never before, humankind is moving to leave the old ways of thinking behind us once and for all.

Everything from the past is being questioned. It's not just the cold war. It's the nation-state system. It's our economic infrastructure. It's our use of the environment. The list goes on. But at the core is a sense that the thinking of the past makes no sense in our "brave new world."

Today, there is a struggle between the new and the old. Many of the old ways of thinking hold on, but for how long? As we discussed earlier, one crisis could push the entire world into an almost unbelievable transformation overnight.

Deiter Heinrich is the executive director of the World Federalists of Canada. Looking at the issue of world government, he summed it up this way:

> The fact that the world as-it-is is not yet ready for world government does not mean that World Federalists are too early with their ideas, or that we should wait while more people change their thinking. . . . Thinking can change very suddenly in the wake of crisis. . . . Obviously we are not

praying for a good crisis, but the likelihood of one in the
absence of world federation is high. We must be ready in
great numbers to push for the necessary changes when things
start shaking loose. This is how evolution occurs, not in a
smooth curve of progression, but in fits of crisis and change.
—Canadian World Federalist Newsletter, February 1985

Once again, imagine the incredible changes that could
suddenly become possible when all of the challenges our
world faces are being amplified by the year 2000. The
world will be perfectly set up for a massive change in
thinking, and one emotional trigger will be enough to set
the whole thing into motion. For the student of God's
Word, it's hard to imagine a world more perfectly
prepared for massive deception than this one. No wonder
Jesus said that if He allowed it, even the strongest of
believers would be deceived.

THE GOSPEL IN THE WORLD OF *STAR TREK*

In a world where thinking is changing and the old is cast
off in favor of the new, it is not hard to imagine how the
world's view of Christianity could suddenly turn far worse
than it already is.

Gene Roddenberry, the creator of *Star Trek*, spelled out
the parameters of the new gospel he was introducing to
the world:

> If the future is not for the faint-hearted, it is even more
> certainly not for the cowardly. . . . Those who insist theirs is
> the only correct government or economic system deserve
> the same contempt as those who insist that they have the
> only true God.
>
> —*Time* magazine, April 18, 1988

Likewise, Mortimer J. Adler, one of the leading thinkers
of our day, a man who helped edit the *Encyclopaedia*

Britannica, foresees that while religion may play a role in the new order, it will have to be slightly modified:

> We have no problem at all if religion does not claim to involve knowledge and it is not concerned with what is true and what is false. If, however, it claims to involve knowledge . . . [and it claims that] it alone has its source in divine revelation, accepted by an act of faith that is in itself divinely caused [and if] . . . religion claims to possess supernatural knowledge— knowledge that man has only as a gift from God . . . then we are confronted with a special problem.
>
> —Mortimer J. Adler, "World Peace in Truth," *Center Magazine,* March 1928

As you can see, we do not have two different views of the future. The gospel of the New Age has no place whatsoever for Christian faith. And while Christian theology is bashed for being divisive, the New Age idea of religion not only rejects Christianity, it opposes any faith that claims to have anything to say about truth or that claims to possess any knowledge whatsoever!

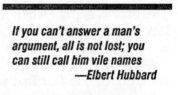

If you can't answer a man's argument, all is not lost; you can still call him vile names
—Elbert Hubbard

IF THEY HATED ME . . .

Of course, none of this comes as a surprise to the student of Bible prophecy. We have already discussed that we believe that the rapture is the very event that is going to trigger the beginning of this global transformation. And we have already said that we believe that it will catapult the Antichrist to world prominence.

But did you know that the Bible even tells us what the first words out of the mouth of the Antichrist will be? That's right, God allowed the apostle John to foresee the

Beast's rise onto the world scene and to actually hear his first words to the world:

> And he opened his mouth in blasphemy against God, to blaspheme his name, and his tabernacle, and them that dwell in heaven. And it was given unto him to make war with the saints. (Rev. 13:6–7)

Thus, the tirades against God that we hear today, are nothing more than a pale foreshadowing of what is to come. But as we pointed out, in our day there are *two* main views of the meaning of the millennium. Let's look at the other.

PROPHECY IS GETTING WHITE HOT

As we approach the year 2000 the interest in Bible prophecy is getting white hot. Why? Is it because people have studied the prophecies of the Bible and are convinced that they are indeed being fulfilled in minute detail? Unfortunately not. Instead, most of the interest comes from one fact that by and large overwhelms every other reason: We are approaching the year 2000.

At every major point in history, people have looked toward the skies believing that theirs is the generation that will see the culmination of world history and the unfolding of God's plan. And, of course, every generation before has been wrong.

While today we're happy to see people thinking about the return of our Lord, it worries us that they are doing so, once again, for all the wrong reasons. Instead of understanding what the Lord has said, they are caught up in the excitement of the turn of the millennium. Have you ever heard the phrase "jumping on the bandwagon"? It happens to sports teams every year during the play-offs. As the momentum builds and the excitement rises, people who have never even followed the team become die-hard fans. Until the end of the season, that is—then, as quickly as they came, they're gone again.

Frankly, we're worried that this is what is happening in the world of Bible prophecy. People are coming on board for the wrong reasons. "So what?" you might ask. After all, if people are on board, does it really matter how they got here?

IN AN HOUR WHEN YOU THINK NOT . . .

Well, let's imagine that the Lord tarries and doesn't return for another five or ten years. How much interest do you think there will be in the Lord's return in 2003 compared to 1999? And, the people who jumped on the millennial bandwagon—only to be disappointed—will be less likely to want to keep watching after having been let down the first time.

Could such a thing happen? Remember what Jesus said about His return? He reminded His true disciples, "Therefore be ye also ready: for in such an hour as ye think *not* the Son of man cometh" (Matt. 24:44, *emphasis added*).

It makes us wonder if the Lord's return may well be sometime *after* the turn of the new millennium. After all, from now until then many, many people will be expecting His coming. Afterward the number will be far less.

It also is of great concern to us that with so many people interested in prophecy for the wrong reasons, every Tom, Dick, and Harry is going to come out with his particular teaching on the subject that may get wide coverage because of the millennial curve. And what a tool for Satan. He can't change the truth of God's prophetic Word, but he can sure try to hide it in a mile-high pile of garbage. We say that to tell you to be very careful about where you get your facts and prophetic teachings over the next few years. And most important, make sure that you understand what the Bible *does* and *does not* say about the end times.

WILL JESUS RETURN IN 2000?

"Wait just a moment!" many will cry. Doesn't the Bible predict that the Lord will return around the year 2000?

This idea, though it smacks of date setting, has gotten wide coverage in the past few years for obvious reasons. Even solid prophetic teachers seem to venture in with various dates and scenarios. In general the idea comes from a couple of biblical passages and one man's calculations.

Most of us know that the book of Genesis teaches that God created the heavens and the earth in six days. He then rested on the seventh day. Some interpreters take that bit of information and then connect it to a passage in the second letter of the apostle Peter where Peter said, "But, beloved, be not ignorant of this one thing, that one day is with the Lord as a thousand years, and a thousand years as one day" (2 Peter 3:8).

Thus, the argument is made that just as the Lord made the earth in six days and rested on the seventh, world history will run for six thousand years, and then the Lord will rule over a one-thousand-year millennium that corresponds to the seventh day, the day of rest.

If that were the case, it would mean that from the year that God created the earth to the year that Jesus returned to establish his kingdom would be six thousand years. But for such a theory to shed light on the year in which the Lord would return, you would need to know the exact year in which the Lord created the earth.

Proponents of this theory point to the calculations made by Archbishop James Usher in the 1600s. Usher used biblical passages and chronologies in an effort to calculate the date for Adam's creation. He concluded that the earth was created in 4004 B.C. A further refinement of calculations concluded that the year was actually 4000 B.C.

That's it. There's where the idea that the Lord will return in roughly the year 2000 comes from. Just take 4000 B.C. and add six thousand years and presto, you've got it. But if it was that simple, why bother with any of the other detailed prophecies the Lord has provided? What do you need them for?

The fact is that this theory cannot be proved. First of all, combining two passages from the Bible in this way, while very interesting, is poor theology. Second, Jewish scholars have done the same study and come up with a completely different date for the creation—they calculate the date to have been 3760 B.C. And finally, if it was that obvious, why did Jesus say that even He did not know the day or hour of His return?

But there's still another problem. For the Lord to establish His kingdom and begin the millennial period in 2000 A.D., the rapture, the rise of the Antichrist, and the seven-year Tribulation would all have to come before then. And we can now say conclusively that none of this happened in 1993.

So, it's all just silliness right? Well, yes, except for one thing. It seems, based on a solid study of Bible prophecy, that our Lord is going to return very, very soon. And if that's true it's going to be at some time not too far from the year 2000! Very interesting, but it's still theologically inadmissible evidence.

Perhaps when the Lord does return, we'll learn the exact date of creation and the changes that have taken place in our calendars since that time. And maybe we'll find out that it was indeed six thousand years from the time of creation until His coming. But for the time being, we'll have to stick to the many solid prophetic signs that the Lord gave us, and recognize that He could well delay His coming until after the year 2000.

HOW SHALL WE THEN LIVE?

How should Christians then live in this climactic moment in history? Should we join the Unabomber and resist new technology? Should we withdraw from society and try to separate ourselves from it?

No. A thousand times no. Now is not the time for climbing hills. Think of the damage done to the cause of Christ by extremist cults. Remember what we said earlier. Satan cannot change the truth, but he can try to bury it in piles of extremism and foolishness that make the world want to run the other way.

God has called us to be the salt of this earth. You can't be the salt if you're up on a mountain somewhere gazing into the sky. That's not going to reach the world. That's going to turn the world off—and rightly so.

Jesus told His disciples very plainly to "occupy till I come" (Luke 19:13). He wants us to be a part of society while being separate from the evils of the world.

We should be productive, contributing members of society. We should look to the future and work, within the confines of our faith, to make this world a better place. My goodness, how is it that Christianity has suddenly become labeled as antienvironment? Because we may oppose those who use the issue of the environment to achieve their own ends, that does not mean that we should forgo protecting God's creation to the best of our ability. We have been given the stewardship of this planet.

At the same time, we need to stand for world peace, though clearly understanding that it is not the same as the peace of Christ. We must understand how fearful we would be if it were not for the grace of God. Apart from that promise of eternal salvation, the only hope this world has is preventing war and protecting the environment. Although we can point to a greater eternal security, we should be understanding of the world's fears and concerns.

We worry about the criticism leveled at students of Bible prophecy. You know the one—"They're so heavenly minded, they're no earthly good." In many instances this rebuke has been earned. We, as Christians, need to be on the cutting edge of technology. We need to be involved in all of the issues of our day if we are to be the salt of this earth.

On the other hand, some Christians have taken it too far the other way. They have rejected the hope of our Lord's return and are trying to build the kingdom here on earth *for* Him. The danger is that such activity reduces the gospel into just another political agenda instead of a message of eternal salvation.

Our philosophy on the matter is pretty basic. We believe in the God of the Bible. We believe that His Son died for our sins and that through faith in Him we can have eternal salvation. And we believe that He is coming soon. So we go about our business every day occupying until He returns. But each day we keep one eye on the sky to remind ourselves that while the world is expecting something big to happen, it is nothing in comparison to what we await!

You Be the Judge

We trust that this book has helped you to see the Bible and its prophecies in an entirely new way. And if you've really read it with an open mind, you've got to admit that the Bible is one amazing book!

How could anyone foretell the future this way? How could you look two thousand or more years into the future and predict that the generation that saw Israel return to her land, after a world dispersion and Holocaust, would also see the greatest leap in knowledge the world has ever seen?

How could you know that this same generation would also build the technology to bring the promise of godhood to life through virtual reality? How could you know that something called television would give the Antichrist a way to reach the world with his false gospel?

Well, as you know, the list goes on. But now you must be the judge. And always remember that even if you choose not to decide, you still have made your choice.

You know we've already shared what it takes to receive eternal salvation. You just have to believe that God is who He says He is. You just have to admit that you are a sinner and believe that Jesus died for your sins. You just have to ask Him to come into your heart and to live there as your Savior.

So, the process is not the hard thing. You can say the right prayer in thirty seconds. But, that's not the hard thing. The hard thing is deciding to say those words with all your heart and your soul. So start a dialogue with God right now that is true and honest. If you can't imagine God existing, tell Him that. If you think things have been too tough in your life to allow you to believe in God, tell Him that. It doesn't matter where you start, just start. And remember this promise: "And ye shall seek me, and find me, when ye shall search for me with all your heart" (Jer. 29:13).